I AM : HERE

I AM:
HERE

*My Faith
Journey
as a Survivor*

Claudia Beasley

Contribution by
Michael Beasley, AbigailWilliams, and Benjamin Williams

XULON PRESS

Xulon Press
2301 Lucien Way #415
Maitland, FL 32751
407.339.4217
www.xulonpress.com

Paperback ISBN-13: 978-1-6628-4501-7
Ebook ISBN-13: 978-1-6628-4688-5

Dedication

This book is dedicated to all the doctors, nurses, staff members, EMT drivers, Life-Flight crew and pilot who were involved in my transports, my hospital admissions and care while in ICU and the Long Term Acute Care Facility. From the cleaning lady in my ICU room who gave me a get well card and prayed for my healing to the doctors, nurses, and specialists; I knew I was in caring hands.

I also want to give recognition to my church family at Grace Community Fellowship in Brenham, Tx and my Life Group and many friends for always covering me in prayer for healing and strength to get well. Without them and my gracious HEAVENLY FATHER listening to prayer I would not be here.

Last but not least by any means I write this book for my family and the support and love they showed me throughout this process of surviving COVID 19.

Preface

I am a 65 year old woman soon to be 66 on October 30, 2021. I was a teacher for 40 years before retiring in December of 2017. I taught in 3 different states Indiana, Nebraska, and Texas. I've taught Kindergarten, Music 1-6, 3rd grade, 4th grade, and 5th grade, my last position as a 5th grade math teacher.

As women, we wear many hats 24/7 switching seamlessly from one to the other without hesitation. We don't realize most days how many different hats we have had to wear throughout the day without thinking; and most days can't figure out why we are so tired.

The chapter titles express the hats I have identified as helpful in my recovery from COVID 19. This book, the title of the book, and the chapter titles have been inspired in me by the LORD. My hope is that you will gain something from reading this and begin to lean in to that voice in your heart.

Chapters

I AM: *A Woman of Faith*

I was transferred from a hospital in College Station, Texas August 14, 2021 after being there since July 15, to an LTAC which is short for Long Term Acute Care facility in New Braunfels, Texas. As I was lying in bed one night during my prayer time, I decided to have a discussion with the LORD. I gave HIM all the praise and glory for bringing me through this life threatening COVID-19 experience. I knew HE wasn't through with me yet; I still had a purpose for being here.

What I didn't know prior to this conversation was the purpose the LORD had for me. I was given this mandate from HIM to write a book about my experience, my faith throughout my life, and my family support. My mind was flooded with the title and the chapter titles, and how I would fill in the gaps of the time line which I have no recollection of; such as being put on a ventilator, taking a Life-Flight to another hospital, being in isolation in the Intensive Care Unit or ICU, being taken off the ventilator and that prognosis. My spirit knew to ask my husband, my daughter, and my son to write their experience from each of their viewpoints for this piece of my time line; to fill in the necessary gaps and be included in my WARRIOR chapter.

Through the years I have always felt the presence of GOD in my life during troubled times, hardships, and always felt directed when needing to make life changing decisions. As hindsight is always 20/20, I can look back over my situations and know that HE was there in the midst of it all.

The first time I recognized my deep faith and protection at work; was when I could not conceive a child in my first marriage. I had met this man between my freshman and sophomore year of college. He was 15 years older than myself. We did wait until I graduated from Hillsdale College in May of 1977 to get married. We married in June of 1977 and divorced in June of 1983. This marriage ended due to my husband's extramarital affair after 6 years of marriage and working with a fertility doctor. The LORD's plan for my future was not with this man. HE had not chosen this man for me; I had picked this one.

My faith was tested many times during my second marriage that lasted 9 years. As I was getting ready to walk down the aisle, I knew I should not marry this man. My biological clock had started ticking loudly in my head and heart and I wanted a family. At the time I felt like this was my only option being 30 years old already. We married in June of 1985 and divorced in April of 1994. I discovered after marriage that this man was addicted to pornography. He brought this evilness into our bedroom. There was no concern for my feelings about it, only his needs were paramount. Towards the end of the marriage, I felt trapped in an unequally yoked marriage. In my first pregnancy I developed pre-eclampsia at 7 months of pregnancy, was rushed into an emergency C-Section, and almost died. My son was born at 28 weeks weighing 3 pounds and 1 ounce with a length of 12 inches on July 2, 1986. My GOD watched over both of us, comforted us, gave us both healing strength. Benjamin moved through the levels of the Neonatal Intensive Care Unit called the NICU quickly; came home 6 weeks later at 34 weeks weighing just under 5 pounds. The peace I felt holding my son in my arms in his bedroom was a peace that was all consuming. A peace that told me I've got you Claudia, in the palm of MY hand, and I won't let you go. During the course of the next several years I had 2 miscarriages. The first one at 10 weeks the second one at 15 weeks. The emotional pain of loss of an unborn child is hard to bear. Knowing I could go to the LORD and pour my heart out to HIM knowing HE could ease my pain, comfort me, and surround me in HIS warm embrace is what got me through those hardships.

My last pregnancy gave me my daughter, Abigail. She was born on May 24, 1991. I started the pre-eclampsia again and had to take a disability leave at 7 months pregnant from my teaching position till the planned C-section in May. My husband had taken a job transfer to Ohio to keep his job. He traveled from

Indiana to Ohio every Sunday and came back every Friday. My parents at the time were full time RV'ers so they moved in with us to help out with my son and see that I got the bed rest I was ordered to do by the doctor. They gave us our family space and went to their 5th wheel trailer each Friday night and came back Sunday night. My parents and I had many nights around the dining room table praying together for this unborn child and for my health for the endurance of the pregnancy. Our prayers were answered with the delivery of a healthy 5 pound 6 ounce, 21 inch baby girl. I had not wanted to know the sex of the baby before delivery since I knew it would be my last pregnancy. I was having my tubes tied after the C-section was completed. I knew deep down I wanted a girl and didn't want to be disappointed knowing it could have been another boy. Again, GOD answered my unspoken prayer since HE knows our deepest desires.

By the fall of 1993 I told my husband I wanted him to find a job back in Indiana to save our marriage. I had begun to dread Friday evenings when I knew he would be returning for the weekend. I found myself looking forward to Sundays when he would be leaving again. I believe to this day that he had an affair while in Ohio. We went to marriage counseling to work on trust issues. The job search began and he moved home in mid-October to start his new job. By that December, I knew I had made a mistake in having him move home. I knew in my heart that this marriage was over. I poured over scripture and prayed for discernment on this decision. It came down to a passage that was shown to me about unions of unequally yoked people. I was a prayerful, faith filled Christian woman he was not a Christian man. We separated in January of 1994 and our divorce was final in April of 1994. My parents started traveling again as I became a single parent of 2 children ages 3 and 8; leaning on the LORD for my support and guidance. Through continued counseling and prayer, I was able to work through the guilt of getting another divorce.

Even though I was divorced from this man, my interactions and needing my faith even more than before happened December 3, 1994 – trial in May of 1997. My ex-husband broke into my home and raped me at gun point. It was a visitation weekend and he had left the kids with his mom to come to my house and commit this act. His final words to me as he left were "I know we won't be able to forget this night, but in time I hope you can forgive me." I called the police after he left, went to the hospital to be checked out, and called my attorney at home to tell him what happened. The attorney said he would work on changing the joint custody paperwork to Sole Custody paperwork but not tell my ex that I had contacted the police. My only prayers at this point were for the safety of my children and their safe return on Sunday evening. The LORD protected my children and returned them home safely on Sunday. I prayed a blessing over them both and cast out any demons that had attached to them in JESUS name! My

ex-husband signed the paperwork giving me sole custody. The police did question him but made no arrests
at that time.

The arrest did not come until March of 1996. This
came after I had been to a 700 Club Singles Conference
the summer of 1995. At that conference I was given an
example for the statement: Forgive and Forget. I felt the
LORD speaking directly to me that whole conference.
Only GOD can forget, humans cannot. The example
given was: "When you get a cut on your hand, it festers,
heals, and leaves a scar. We as humans can't say the cut
never happened. But we can say we are healed from the
pain that the cut caused." Those words really had an
impact on me. GOD had used this message to soften my
heart. I had felt led to write a book about my unequally
yoked marriage, divorce, and rape. It was titled "Healed
by The Master's Hand" (never published). In March of
1996 during my prayer time and writing of that book I
said out loud, "GOD, if my not forgiving my ex-husband is preventing his arrest help me to say those words."
I said them aloud using the cut hand and scar example
from the conference. I said, "I forgive you for the pain
you caused me when you raped me." I continued with,
"You no longer have power and control over my life."
The very next day I got a call from the lead detective to
tell me that they had arrested my ex, had taken a lot of
evidence from his home, and he was being booked on
a Felony A assault with a deadly weapon. The LORD

DOES answer prayer when we pray from our hearts and are sincere in our desires.

The trial was in May of 1997 and lasted 2 days which were very grueling, painful, and frustrating. I had brought some praise music tapes to listen to as the jury deliberated. The prosecutor had arranged with the judge ahead of time to remand my ex till the sentencing hearing if he was found guilty. He had made threats to harm me and my other family members. As I listened to the words of GOD's promises in the praise music, I felt a calm and peace wash over me. I knew HE had my back no matter what the outcome. As we got word the jury was back the Prosecutor advised us before the jury came in that it didn't look good; there were no bailiffs in the courtroom. Bailiffs would be taking my ex into custody if it was a guilty verdict. The LORD was preparing me for a Not Guilty verdict! When the jury read the verdict Not Guilty there was an uproar in the courtroom from the defense table. After the jury was dismissed, the Judge said, "I believe your ex-wife, you did it, and you will do it again. Case dismissed." He pounded the gavel, got up, and walked out. I felt vindicated and knew in my heart that everything would be okay. The bailiffs agreed with the Judge and said as much as they offered to walk us to our car as a precaution.

It was the summer of 1998 a year after the trial and I wanted to move out of Indiana to Texas. I had no family in the mid-west anymore, both brothers were in Texas and my parents travel the southern states during the winter months. During my devotions one night I very distinctly heard a voice in my spirit say "MOVE". I went to my living room and told my parents that I was going to move to Texas. We needed to start packing, so I could put the house on the market, sell, and move. I would need to meet with my ex-husband and his attorney to get permission to move out of state and work out visitation rights for extended visits. The LORD can move mountains when HE wants to. I met with my attorney ahead of our meeting with my ex and his attorney. I outlined what I wanted and needed. I also told him to let the other attorney know up front that I wanted to say something to my ex before we adjourned. As the LORD promised to have my back, to give me the desires of my heart HE was there in that room giving me strength and providing for me. I got everything that I had asked for as far as moving and visitations. What I was finally able to say to my ex in person was, "Remember that night in December of 1994 when you broke into my house and raped me at gunpoint? I want you to know that in March of 1996 I forgave you for the pain you caused me and you don't have power or control over me anymore." I could visibly see a change come over my ex's face and a sinking into his chair. He was defeated. GOD is good all the time, all the time GOD is good. I sold my house in 8 days and moved to Texas in July of 1998. As a side note, I picked this husband too, not GOD, but HE still didn't forsake me. My faith saw me through this unequally yoked 9 year marriage.

I began my new life as a single woman with 2 children in Corpus Christi, Texas. Once again, my parents gave up traveling to help me move and get settled. I could not find a teaching position in Corpus Christi so I began interviewing in the Houston, Texas area. My parents stayed with my kids in Corpus while I stayed with my brother in Houston for interviews. I was able to land a 2nd semester Reading teacher position at a Middle School. Next on the agenda was to find a house. After a short search I found and closed on a house and my parents packed up the 2 bedroom apartment and storage unit and brought everything up to the new house in Pecan Grove located in Richmond, Texas. My parents were always such a blessing to me and to my children.

It was February 1999 and I was still single after 5 years. I didn't start looking at dating until April 2000. I took the lead on this again instead of waiting on the LORD to bring me my soulmate. It had been 6 years of single life and I thought I was ready for a partner. I didn't however pray about it first. I'm heading into another faith journey!! I met my future 3rd husband at Easter time. He was great with both of the kids. He seemed like a great role model for my son, encouraged him in sports, helped him make the football team in Middle School. He was like a rock for me and seemed so solid. He knew what to say and do, so I just let him be the Head of our little family. We married in

January of 2001 and it lasted 5 years until we divorced in April 2006.

Number 3 moved us to Nebraska away from all family and friends in the summer of 2001, when he took a new job. I had to take a $15,000 pay cut for the teaching job I found with Omaha Public Schools. With no family or friends my husband became the center of all things. I was feeling very isolated. I finally found a church to attend and made friends there. I think that was part of the downfall of the marriage. He said he was a Christian but his actions did not support that. A familiar pattern of unequally yoked kept cropping up in my mind. The LORD has a way of talking to you when you are still and can listen with your heart. In the summer of 2004, he lost his job in Nebraska and couldn't seem to find anything. I asked if I could look back in Texas since I could make more money there. I began searching and interviewing staying with my brother in Houston again. I took a 5th grade Math position with Houston Independent School District and began in the fall of 2004. Abigail stayed with #3 in Nebraska going to school, waiting for the house to sell, and then move back to Texas to restart our family life here.

We were a family again in May 2005 when we sold our Nebraska home and bought our Texas home. By October of 2005 our marriage had disintegrated. Actions by my husband totally violated our marriage vows and trust. It was totally obvious once again that I had been unequally yoked in marriage. I filed for divorce but he contested it. Our divorce was finalized by a Judge in court due to the criminal charges that had been filed on my soon to be ex-husband. Both my attorney and the Judge told me directly that, "I had a bad picker and needed to figure out why I choose mates so poorly." I knew the answer to that. I had not waited on the LORD to bring me my soulmate and helpmate whom HE had chosen for me. HIS preparations for each of us had not been completed yet. I had sought out partners on my own not prayerfully seeking HIM and HIS plan for my life partner and mate.

I AM: *A Wife*

*F*or me the months after my 3rd divorce were filled with grief of lost relationships and guilt for having 3 failed marriages as a Christian woman. I had put my children through two divorces; one being from their father. I did a lot of soul searching and praying for wisdom to find the cause or reason that I had a bad picker. I had been searching for someone to make me complete. I had to learn that 1(one) is a whole number. I needed to become comfortable with myself, by myself, and not look for someone to fill that hole. My whole life I had put others before myself, I always came last. This thinking needed to change. As women we all have a tendency to do this to ourselves. We put our family and job needs ahead of our own needs. This whole concept would turn my world upside down, making me focus on myself instead of others.

During one of my quiet times with the LORD I felt a nudging question from my spirit, "What makes you happy?" I really had to stop and think about that. I had not found a church to attend since my divorce in the spring of 2006. Getting involved with a church, getting back to singing in a choir and or Praise Team, making new Christian friends through small group or Sunday School became a new focus for me. I began attending Kingsland Baptist Church. There was a wonderful choir that I joined as well as a Praise Team and I began to feel refreshed and happy with myself and life in general. The church had a Singles Sunday School class that also did things socially together. I was finally able to make new friends that were like minded Christians. Life was good. "What else made me happy" I asked myself. I wanted to learn how to country western dance and jitterbug. I enrolled in some Country Western 2 step classes and an East Coast Swing class. My holes were being filled and I was happy with me; I felt like a complete person.

In January of 2010 I told the LORD I was swearing off all men. I would not look on my own, I would be content with my singleness. It was shortly after this commitment to GOD that a gentleman named Michael started coming to our singles class and social functions. I found out that he actually attended St. Peter's Methodist next door for services but they didn't have anything for singles at his church. I felt an attraction towards him but I pushed it out of my mind since I had just recently sworn off all men and would be content being single. The LORD was not having it. We started interacting at the single's social functions. Michael and I became friends on Facebook. We would like each other's posts occasionally or write simple funny comments which went on for several months.

Finally in May of 2010, I asked a friend of mine from the singles group if I should reach out and email Michael. He had recently posted on Facebook about going on a wine trail. I was considering asking if he would be interested in going out for a glass of wine. I told her of my commitment to remain single and be happy, that I would not go out searching for another relationship. The LORD does have a sense of humor though. As soon as I gave HIM control over that part of my life, along came Michael! My friend encouraged me to email him which I did. He emailed immediately back that yes, he would love to have a glass of wine with me.

On May 16, 2010 Michael and I had our first date. We have been together ever since. I found out that night that he was a widower since December 2006. He had married his high school sweetheart, Leslie, and had been married for almost 30 years. Leslie had gotten breast cancer in the later years of their marriage. She had beat it but it came back as lung and brain cancer. She had passed away on Christmas in 2006. Michael had 2 children both grown and out of the house. His son Matthew had recently bought a house a couple of streets over in the same neighborhood. His daughter Allyson had moved to Austin and was living in an apartment with a roommate. I discovered through our conversation that we actually lived in the same subdivision, just a few streets apart. Coincidence, I think not!! Again, the LORD knew what HE was doing when HE brought us together. I thought for sure once I shared about the number of divorces, I had that I would not hear from him again. We talked for a couple hours at the winery and another hour in my driveway. We said our good-byes and I thought that was it, done.

Michael is a very shy and quiet person. We emailed several times after our first "date". He asked me out for dinner and a movie. I invited him over to watch a movie one night. I asked if he liked to Country Western dance and he said it had been years but yes, he did. We went dancing and just clicked. We even signed up together for several different levels of Country Western 2-step and Country Waltz lessons. Michael has a great sense of humor, is fun to be around, and very conservative. I felt so comfortable around him and could totally be myself. He introduced me to his children over a dinner at his house. We all played a card game together called International Rummy which is a family favorite of theirs. It was a few weeks of dating and we started introducing each other to our groups of friends. There were two groups of friends that I was introduced to. There was his church group of friends from St. Peter's and his neighborhood friends all of which knew his deceased wife, Leslie. I think he needed their reassurance that this was okay, that I fit in, and he should pursue the relationship. I introduced Michael to both of my children and they hit it off as well. Small dinner parties at my house with my friends were a success also.

Several more weeks passed and Michael invited me for a weekend at his friends' cabin near Lake Somerville. It was a lovely weekend. The conversation on the way home got intense. He told me out of the blue, "Under no circumstances will I ever get married again." I retorted with, "I've been down that road too many times and I wouldn't get married again either!!" We were both fighting the LORD's plan for us to be together. We continued dating and continued growing closer and closer together.

We began traveling together. Our first trip was to Michigan to meet my 3 high school friends I have kept in contact with. Another trip was San Francisco and the Napa Valley. Michael took me to his high school reunion, to his niece's wedding in Tennessee and then on to North and South Carolina to see an old friend of his. I attended his son's wedding and also his daughter's wedding. I still felt awkward at family gatherings since I really wasn't "part of the family" not being married to Michael. Everyone always made an effort to include me but it just wasn't the same. I said the "I love you" to Michael first, it was a couple more years before he let it slip out when he thought I couldn't hear him. He knows now that I have fine-tuned hearing!

Michael and I dated for 6 years before we got married on July 16, 2016. We were truly best friends and companions before we got married. GOD's plan is always the best plan for you. I just had to let go and let GOD take over in this part of my life. Michael is truly my soulmate and helpmate. I cannot imagine my life without him. We were two complete and whole people who wanted to share their lives with someone else. The LORD brought us together in HIS perfect timing. My advice to anyone now is "Wait upon the LORD" and "Let HIM know the desires of your heart".

Our wedding was perfect!! We got married at The Swinging Door a BBQ place in Richmond, Texas. We rented the large back room that had a space for the ceremony, the reception, and dancing. One of my dear friends from school offered to do all the flowers and decorations for the wedding as her gift. She made table cloths, flower boxes for the tables, the bouquets for the girls and boutonnieres for the guys. My brother, Stephen, performed the marriage ceremony. Allyson and Abigail were my attendants and Matthew and Benjamin were Michael's attendants. My Dad was actually able to walk me down the aisle after having heart surgery 6 weeks before hand. We wrote our own vows to each other which were very sweet. My brother talked us through a sand ceremony where we had 3 colors of sand and white. The white represented the LORD's foundation of our marriage and was at the bottom of the container. Michael then added his green sand and then I added my melon colored sand. Benjamin and Abigail added the yellow sand of the children. Then Michael's green and my melon sand followed by Matthew and Sarah's yellow sand. The final layer was Michael's green and my melon sand followed by Allyson and Brandon's

yellow sand. The very top layer was white again representing the LORD's head of our family. These grains
of sand can never be removed as they are all blended
together as one under the LORD's blessing. I still have
this container with our wedding date and two entwined
hearts engraved on the front sitting on my mantle along
with several wedding pictures from that day. One of my
student's parent was a photographer and offered to do
our wedding pictures as her gift to us. The pictures are
fabulous. I have my album sitting on my coffee table
as I write this book. Michael and I learned a country
waltz dance to a song he found on the internet. It spoke
of GOD's plan, our meeting, and relationship to a tee.
Our first dance as a married couple was an amazing
success. Our wedding was so much fun and so many
relationships were represented that night. Family from
all sides were there, friends from both of our places of
work, church friends, neighborhood friends, and even
friends from Nebraska came down to partake in the
celebration. From the BBQ to the cupcakes fun was
had by all.

We missed our 5 year anniversary since I was on a
ventilator in the ICU in College Station. I of course did
not know any of this. I do know that when the doctors
brought me out of my drug induced sedation, he was
the first person I wanted to see. We held hands constantly. He stayed overnight in the hospital with me
even though he had to get special permission daily to do
so. Michael started filling in the missing pieces of the

timeline going to the hospital to coming off the ventilator. My daughter told me that the day they put me on the ventilator was the day before our anniversary. The doctors took me off the ventilator 2 weeks after our 5 year wedding anniversary. From that piece of information, I know for sure that GOD had HIS hand in my survival. Michael had lost his wife due to cancer on Christmas in 2006. He had a very difficult time every Christmas after that. He would not decorate, have a tree, or participate in any celebrations because the day was too much of a painful reminder of her passing. Michael knows the LORD. I know that Michael could not have taken another spouse passing around another time of celebration. The LORD held us both in the palm of HIS hand that day and brought me out of the grips of death to be with Michael again. I do know that I was not and am not ready to be separated in death from Michael. He was my advocate and supporter through this whole ordeal. GOD put him in my life for this very reason as GOD knows HIS plans for me.

I love Michael with my whole being. I'm so glad I gave this part of my life over to GOD. Having faith and feeling the loving support from Michael, family, friends, and GOD Himself got me through this COVID-19 battle. I came home 2 days shy of being in a hospital setting for 2 months. Michael's love for me and commitment to me never wavered. I am a wife to the most amazing husband a woman could ever want or have. I am blessed to have him in my life and I am so thankful to GOD for bringing us together. We are still going strong and had a little post anniversary gift exchange here at the house. I had forgotten about ordering his gift before I got sick. He of course had not. It was a perfect day to celebrate our life together again in our home. It was September 9, 2021 the morning after my return home. We were sitting on the couch having our morning coffee, watching the news, and holding hands. It was at this point that he turned to me with tears in his eyes. He told me he loved me so much and had been afraid he wouldn't be able to enjoy this morning routine with me ever again. Michael asked if I would like to exchange anniversary gifts. I received a beautiful marriage plaque and I gave him a Best Husband since 2016 t-shirt. Both were simple in thought but so deeply meaningful.

I felt my hats as a woman of faith and a wife firmly in place and secure. My faith hat is worn daily and securely knowing that HE is with me every step, every decision, and every breath that I take. Giving HIM total control over my life took time, but once I did, I have been blessed many times over.

I AM: *A Mother*

*O*ne of the greatest gifts that comes from GOD is the gift of a child. I was blessed with this gift twice in my life giving birth to a son and a daughter; they have blessed me beyond measure. I am so proud of them and the fine adults they have become.

Since I had difficulty getting pregnant in my first marriage I was totally surprised when I got a positive pregnancy test in my second marriage. The LORD did know the desires of my heart to have children. It was my biological clock ticking that had gotten me down the aisle to marry this man. I was given an August 17,1986 due date. My marriage at that time was a little rocky and surviving on shaky ground. My husband was addicted to pornography. I started going to counseling because I felt my self-esteem going down and down. I went to all of my doctor appointments alone; we would verbally fight before going to every birthing class.

It was at my 7 month appointment on Friday June 27 that my husband decided to go with me; since he would be leaving for 2 weeks Army Reserves training as a Drill Sergeant the following morning. At this appointment my blood pressure was elevated and I was putting out protein in my urine sample. The doctor was concerned that I may be developing preeclampsia. I was told to go home, have complete bed rest, and return Monday June 30. If there was not significant improvement I would have to be admitted to the hospital for the duration of the pregnancy. With my husband leaving the following day my mother came down to stay with me and drive me to the doctor appointment on Monday.

I followed doctor's orders and my mom's all weekend. The weird thing about all of this was I felt perfectly fine. Mom and I prayed together for a good report on Monday before leaving the townhouse. My blood pressure was even higher at 180/100. Mom took me straight over to the hospital to have a stress test done on the baby. I still did not know if I was having a boy or a girl. After the test I was admitted. Mom was my rock during all of this. My Dad flew down from Grand Rapids, Michigan to Fort Wayne, Indiana the next day. I remember having a horrible headache circling my head and squeezing it like a huge vice; tightening more and more. My Dad stood by my bedside and constantly rubbed my head. My doctor had called in an Obstetrician Specialist to take over the case. He informed me that they would need to do a C-section as my blood pressure was still rising and my kidneys could shut down. He contacted the American Red Cross to get a hold of my husband to get an emergency flight home to get there in time for the surgery. My blood pressure had gotten to 200/180 I was near stroke and comma levels. I was rushed to the OR put under at 12:25 AM and my son was born at 12:28 AM on July 2, 1986. He weighed 3 pounds 1 ounce and was 12 inches long. I awoke in the recovery room to my husband's snoring.

I was a mess the next day. I blamed myself for having a premature birth. I should have eaten better, I should have exercised more, I caused the stress to my unborn child with the state of my marriage. GOD was not having any of these thoughts! HE made sure I was able to see my baby in the NICU the following day. I was wheeled down in a wheel chair to sit in front of his incubator. He was so small and frail looking. I just started silently crying when I saw him. Dr. Lewis the head of the NICU came over and saw me. He was a huge man. He asked me, "Have you held your son yet?" I said, "No" and before I knew it this giant of a man had swaddled my tiny little son and put him in my arms tubes and all. He reaffirmed to me what the LORD already knew. "This is not your fault. You did not cause this to happen by any actions you took or didn't take. Preeclampsia is the body's way of dealing with what it considers a "foreign object"."

We finally named our son a few days after his arrival. We couldn't seem to agree on anything so my husband took our choices to the nurses' station and asked them to vote. The name that got voted on the most was Benjamin Michael Joseph. That is a big name for such a little guy. I was discharged from the hospital after a week but Benjamin had to stay in the NICU to get bigger and stronger. I couldn't drive for 4 weeks due to the C-section, so I had to wait till my husband got home from work to drive us to the hospital to see Benjamin and hear about his progress through the day. I know the LORD was with him all the time because he progressed through all the levels of the NICU in rapid succession passing milestone after milestone.

We finally brought him home on August 8, 1986 weighing just under 5 pounds. My parents were there to hold their first Grandchild, a Grandson, for the first time as well. It was a blessing that warms my heart to this day when I think about it; seeing them be able to experience this moment. From that day to the day that both my parents passed on to glory they both had a special bond and relationship with Benjamin. I thank GOD every day for the memories that were created and pressed into our hearts.

My son, Benjamin, is now 35 years old. He has his own family now. Benjamin is married and has 5 sons. Michael is 15, Adam and step-son David are 14, William is 10, and the youngest Benjamin Jr. whom I call BT, is 4 years old. I am so proud of the man, father, and husband he has become. He started working on a 2 year Associates Degree from San Jacinto Community College in Business Administration in the fall of 2020. He will be finished this December 2021 finishing in just 16 months all while working a full time job as the manager of Kwik Kar. He has already been accepted by University of Houston to complete his Bachelor of Science Degree in Business Management beginning in January of 2022. Benjamin asked to be put on the fast track to graduate in May of 2023. This would again be a huge milestone completed in just a year and a half. He is also considering continuing his education with a Master's Degree from Texas A&M.

The LORD had his hand on Benjamin during his adolescent years keeping him safe and protected. He was in my prayers constantly. As Benjamin established himself as a family man, I prayed for him to find a church to network with likeminded people. To make new friends with his wife and help his sons grow up with the knowledge of GOD and how HE plays a role in each of their lives. After going through this COVID-19 experience with me Benjamin turned to the LORD and found strength and peace in HIS presence. I am very happy to say that the LORD heard my prayers and answered them in a mighty way. Benjamin took his entire family to church, has gotten his wife involved with a women's Bible study group on Mondays, the teenagers go to Teen Bible study on Wednesdays, and he attends a Men's Bible study on Thursdays. Will, the 10 year old says church is fun and he has even made a new friend! Everyone seems to be enjoying the praise and worship time as well as the teaching of the word. Praise be to GOD!!

The birth of my daughter, Abigail, on May 24, 1991 was another miracle story. In between Benjamin's and

Abigail's birth I had 2 miscarriages. The first one was at 10 weeks and I had not heard the heartbeat yet which alerted the doctor to a problem. I underwent an internal ultrasound and found that the tissue was not viable so I had a D&C. My second miscarriage was at 15 weeks and I had heard the heartbeat. I started spotting and we checked for heartbeat after a week; I had lost this baby as well which ended in another D&C. If I didn't have my faith to lean on, I don't know what I would have done or how I would have been able to handle a second loss.

I was between 12 and 15 weeks pregnant with my 4th and final pregnancy when I started bleeding quite heavily. I called the doctor and all they could tell me to do was go to bed, lay on my left side, and come in the following week for a blood test to determine if I was still pregnant. I went in for the test and called to get the results the following day. My hormone levels still said I was pregnant. I said, "I couldn't be, I had bled too much." They said I could come in for an ultra sound to check for heartbeat if I wanted to. I prayed to GOD all the way to their office. I told HIM I could not go through this again, I could not lose this baby. I was heartbroken at the prospect.

I got to the office and they started the ultrasound. We heard the heartbeat and could see it immediately on the screen. The tech moved around the uterus looking for anything unusual that could have been the cause of the bleeding. She did find a small tear in the lining that she said could have been a twin that was lost in the bleeding. The LORD was with me and heard my pleas for help and comfort. Again, GOD is so good to me.

At 7 months I again started developing preeclampsia symptoms and was told I had to take disability from my teaching position for the last 2 months of my pregnancy. I was willing to do anything to get to the planned C-section date and tube tying. I had come to accept the fact that my body apparently did not like being pregnant even though I did. With my husband working during the week in Ohio and driving home on weekends to Indiana I was blessed once again that my parents were in a position to come help me with Benjamin and my need for bed rest. The LORD provides a way for HIS children young and old.

I wanted to be awake for this C-section so I had an epidural to be able to hear the baby and see the baby right away. It was a good thing that we had a planned C-section because this little one was feet and butt down. We had decided on a girl name and boy name ahead of time this time. The doctor announced it was a girl and I cried out in joy, "Thank you JESUS!!" I knew this would be my last pregnancy and I had not wanted another boy. I wanted a little girl to have the kind of special relationship and bond that my mom and I had. The LORD new the desires of my heart and blessed me with a healthy 5 pound 6 ounce 21 inch daughter named Abigail Nicole on May 24, 1991 at 8:38 AM.

Bringing Abigail home with me when I was discharged was such a different experience than what I had with Benjamin. I had come home empty handed, but this time I had a pink bundle of joy to hold and rock and show to Benjamin the big brother. My heart was overflowing. My life felt complete now, I was a mother.

Today my daughter, Abigail is 30 years old. She is an RN-BSN for the ER at a Level 2 Trauma Center in Walnut Creek, California. I am so proud of the young woman she has become. She is smart, witty, loving, goal oriented, and loves the LORD. Abigail worked hard for her degrees and paid for the RN and BSN degrees on her own. I started her off with a Medical Assistant degree. She first worked in the Houston area for a couple of years. She wanted to be a travel nurse and explored her options. Her first assignment was from October to the end of December of 2019 in Raton, New Mexico. She lived in an Air B&B just over the border in Colorado. This girl had never driven in snow before. She always works the night shift. I was a nervous wreck the entire time she was there especially when she said the pass through the mountains, she had to take can shut down due to snow drifts! Second morning there she had to follow a snow plow to get home. Her second assignment was in Walnut Creek, California. Her assignment started in January of 2020 and was supposed to end in March. The hospital asked her to extend another 3 months, and then again and again. They talked to her about going full time regular staff. It wasn't until the

IRS contacted her recruiter and said she could not extend again and be considered a travel nurse since she had worked there a full year. So, Abigail decided to go full time staff plus she had met a guy back in February of 2020 and they were getting serious.

Abigail and her boyfriend Adrian came back to Texas in May of 2021 to collect her furniture and all her belongings from storage and move them back to California. She got herself a 2 bedroom apartment back in March of 2021 and still needed her furniture to complete it. It was sad to see her go permanently but I know she is happy where she is. She does get homesick for me about every 3 months so one of us is flying back and forth to get a mom fix or an Abigail fix.

Due to her crazy night schedule and not being a fixed schedule till recently Abigail had not been able to get involved with a church and make new friends that are like minded Christians. After her schedule was more fixed and she would have Sundays off I started looking for churches in her area online. I found a couple and sent the information. Abigail is like me; we are very grounded in our faith but we miss corporate worship with fellow believers. I have been praying for her to find a local church that she and maybe even Adrian would like and participate in. This whole ordeal with me and fighting my COVID-19 battle has opened her heart to GOD again. After her last visit home to see me, she told me that she had listened to the sermon online for one of the churches I had found. Since Adrian had recently started looking for different employment, she suggested that he listen to it as well. It was about doors closing before new ones can open. Imagine that!! Adrian listened and liked it. The two of them have gone several Sundays in a row now. Praise GOD!! HE continues to have me and my family in the palm of HIS hand guiding us, leading us, and speaking to us.

I love my mom hat. This hat is also infused with my faith hat and has seen me through many times of trial, tribulation, and celebration. Have you identified your hats yet? Men and women have hats though different from one another. Think about your life and how GOD has intervened through HIS love for you.

I AM: *A Step-Mother and Mother-in-law*

*M*ichael has two children his son, Matthew and his daughter, Allyson. I was introduced early on in our relationship to both of them. It was awkward at first, but as the years went by it became more natural. I was Michael's companion/partner for 6 years before getting married and becoming an "official" step-mother. I had made it very clear to both of them from the beginning that I was not there to take their mother's place; I just wanted to be a good close friend that they could come to, confide in, and learn to love. I prayed a lot in the early days of building a relationship with both of them. I asked for guidance, wisdom, what words to say and how to say them. During this same period of time, I met the future spouses for Matthew and Allyson. Again, the Mother-in-law hat did not fit until after Michael and I were married July 16 of 2016. Matthew and Sarah were married August 14, 2015 and Allyson and Brandon were married May 20, 2016.

My son, Benjamin, married Maria on June 23, 2016 a month before Michael and I were married. Benjamin never told me about his marriage till August of 2016 when he came to help me set up my classroom before school started. He explained to me that he didn't want to take away from my excitement of my upcoming wedding in July. So, my mother-in-law hat would be expanded again after my marriage to Michael.

I was included in the festivities of Matthew and Sarah's wedding. We went to cake tasting as his "parents" along with her parents. I sat in the front row with Michael during the wedding with other family members on the groom's side of the aisle. Picture taking was a bit awkward since I wasn't a mother or step-mother. The photographer hadn't been filled in apparently because she kept asking me to come up for the group pictures. The reception went smoothly and Allyson filled in for the mother- son traditional dance.

Allyson and Brandon's wedding was an outdoor affair. I had been included when looking at the venue along with Brandon's Dad and Step-Mom, Kay. This was the first time we had met the other side of the soon to be family. Michael and I helped to decorate the barn where the reception would be held and the outdoor chapel area where the wedding would take place. As father of the bride, he had many more responsibilities to attend to than he did for Matthew's wedding. I think because Michael and I were recently engaged to be married 2 months after Allyson the group pictures for the wedding weren't as awkward. Brandon was always calling me in for a group shot.

As I took on the official role of Step-Mother and Mother-in-law after my marriage to Michael my relationship with Matthew and Sarah seemed to go smoothly and seamlessly. I felt accepted as a member of the family. With Allyson it seemed to be on the superficial level while with Brandon I felt included. Allyson had been very close to her mother prior to losing her and still was grieving her passing from 10 years before. She has a close relationship with her dad and I think she felt threatened by my position in his life. I was not willing to give up on having a close friendship with Allyson. I continued to ask GOD how to communicate with her, how to phrase my words when communicating in person or text. I always cleared my communications with Michael to make sure I wasn't crossing any lines.

My relationship with Allyson now is strong and loving, flowing freely between us. It is now 15 years since her mom passed. I feel a real connection to her and I sense she has a special bond to me as well. I remember how I felt when she said "I love you" and not just "love you too". I believe this stemmed from my personal experiences of miscarriage as she miscarried 3 times. I knew what to say and spoke from my heart and personal knowledge of what she was going through. I felt shear appreciation from Allyson as she was dealing with all of her emotions. When she became pregnant with Scarlett, I wrote her a special note in her Christmas card along with the baby sandals I had made for her. I sent her a text near her birthday in January of

2020 and I told her I would like to be there for her as much as she needed me to be. I shared that my own daughter did not want to have children and I would miss out on that experience with my own daughter. I told her I hoped that she would share this pregnancy with me and that this grandchild could bring us closer together and deepen our relationship. I got a hug emoji, a smile emoji, and yes, she would love that. I feel she and I have bonded while going through this COVID-19 experience. Allyson made a surprise visit to me while I was in the LTAC in New Braunfels. She brought a small bouquet of tulips which brightened my room. I felt the compassion, care, and concern from Allyson as we spoke. We have a special connection now. I see Allyson as my daughter now, not just a step-daughter. The LORD was faithful to the desires of my heart in regards to Allyson.

I have become very close to all of my step-children and in-laws. Michael and I had a blended family as of July 16, 2016. We were talking after I came home about the family. We both agreed that through this COVID-19 experience our family has grown closer, that we had gone from kids and step-kids, my kids and your kids, to just saying "our kids". They had been reaching out to each other for updates and talking more than they ever had. Thank you, JESUS, for all my children. My children are one of the reasons I am still here. Wanting to be a part of their lives and seeing them all grow was my inspiration to fight to get better.

Every day I wear a heart shaped necklace with the birthstones of every month representing all of my children and grandchildren. I absolutely love it and will gladly add more stones for any months not covered already in case there are more grandchildren. This hat is securely in place and not going anywhere.

I AM: *A Sister*

I am the oldest of 3 siblings each of us being 2 years apart. I have 2 younger brothers. My middle brother, Mark, who is currently 64 lives in Houston, Texas and my youngest brother, Stephen, who is currently 62 lives in Corpus Christi, Texas. We were all born in Indiana and grew up in Grand Rapids, Michigan. Mark moved to Texas first. Stephen moved to Long Beach, CA and then settled in Corpus Christi where he still lives today.

My relationships with both my brothers are close. We all deal with the pecking order of our births. Being the oldest came with the most responsibility and my parents leaning on me as the oldest. The middle brother, Mark came with his own pecking order issues. He was definitely the rebel of the 3 of us, trying to get attention. The youngest brother, Stephen had the regrettable stigma of being the baby of the family. I was the rule follower, Mark the rebel, and Stephen probably the smartest by watching both of us and not making our same mistakes.

After our mother passed in 2007, I seemed to take on the role of Matriarch of the family. She had always planned the family gatherings, holiday celebrations, birthdays etc. I just seemed to fall into this role and continue today to try and have both brothers and all family come to my home. It is such a satisfying feeling to be around them both. There is always so much laughter and love that permeates our surroundings. We have the shared memories that we can reminisce on when we get together. This always entails a lot of laughter and smiles. All three of us have the "Isenhour" smile where our eyes are squinting. It is a family trait that we have all come to love. You can definitely tell we are siblings.

All of us grew up in a faith based Christian home. When we were in high school, we were attending a Methodist Church that put on plays and religious reenactments. Mark had a strong faith and even carried his Bible to school each day. I remember one Good Friday the church did a reenactment of the crucifixion and Mark played JESUS CHRIST. Mark carried in a cross on his back, was fastened to the cross, and limply hung on the cross after he uttered his final words "It is done". It was very moving and powerful.

Mark decided to join a Christian traveling theater group called Covenant Players. We had hosted several cast members in our home for meals and sleeping. It turned out to be a very eye opening experience for Mark. There were many times they went hungry, weren't paid, or have places to sleep. Because of this treatment by people who called themselves Christians, Mark turned away from his faith feeling that all Christians were hypocrites. It is my prayer now that Christians cross his path daily and through their actions and words Mark can see that not all Christians are hypocrites. Every day in my prayers I include Mark that he may return and believe that JESUS is the Son of GOD and is the only way to receive eternal life and be reunited with our parents and all of the family one day. He seems to be getting "spiritual" these days which I believe will lead him back.

Stephen has used his love of music to pursue his Christian faith. He plays the keyboard for his church praise team, and is helping to plant another church. At our Mother's Memorial Service, he preached a good sermon. He was willing to get an online pastor license to perform my marriage to Michael. After my mom's passing, I was in charge of my dad's medical, financial, and care needs. I did this from June 2007 – October of 2018. At this point in time Dad needed more round the clock care and attention. Stephen had always said when it was time, he would have Dad live with him. Mark, Stephen, and I had the conversation that it was indeed time. Stephen and his wife opened their home to Dad where he lived until passing there in September of 2019. Stephen relied on his faith in taking care of Dad. I prayed that Stephen would have the strength, compassion, and stamina to look after Dad. He did an excellent job. For Stephen I continue to pray for a deepening of faith that has been well established.

I love both of my brothers so much. I am not ready to leave them on this side to wait for their arrival on the other side. I know I will see Stephen again, but I need to be here for a while to make certain that Mark will be joining us. I want to continue to fight for our souls. My sister hat along with my faith hat are on full alert duty. I pray for my words and actions to impact my brother Mark in a positive way.

I AM: *A Grandmother*

*N*othing in the world compares to being a Grandparent. I saw the relationship each of my children had with each of their Grandparents as they were growing up. There were many times during my single parent days that my parents helped to stand in the gap. I couldn't imagine being a Grandparent myself at that stage of my life. I prayed that I could be as good a grandparent as my parents had been.

I had never seen myself in the role of being a grandmother until it presented itself when my son introduced me to his 2 first born sons, Michael and Adam. I didn't meet them until they were 6 and 5, respectfully, at a visitation center arranged by the court. The Mom had not been letting Benjamin see the boys so the court intervened and set up a neutral location run by the court system for visitation to be able to occur. Benjamin had to arrive 20 minutes before the boys were dropped off and had to leave 20 minutes before the boys were picked up. I was invited to come to one of his visitations in the fall of 2012. I had missed out on the boys being babies and entering their lives as a grandmother. These

Grandsons were born in March of 2006 and 2007. It felt odd and strange to even realize that these were my son's flesh and blood. Coming on the scene this late into their lives seemed like an insurmountable task. My prayer was to be able to open my heart to these little boys and to be able to have some kind of relationship with them however limited that would be. My daughter, Benjamin, and I were able to spend Christmas Day with them that year for the first time in their young lives. We lavished gifts and attention on them and I could tell by the smiles and genuine look of happiness that they enjoyed our time together. It was very heartwarming.

The fall of 2013 Benjamin showed up at my school during the first day back teachers' meeting. When I saw him standing at the doorway, I noticed he was holding his son, Will, 2 years old at the time in his arms. Benjamin was frantic and in tears. He needed my help. Benjamin had received a call that morning to come get Will before CPS came to take him away. The father of Will's mother, had found her strung out on drugs again, not taking care of Will at all. Benjamin was beside himself not knowing what to do. He didn't have a way of paying for daycare for Will since he was working 6 days a week and paying child support on the other two. This was the first time I had laid eyes on Will. He had been born in California and recently returned to Texas. My silent prayer at that moment was HELP LORD!! I took Will into my arms, told Benjamin I would figure it out, and not to worry. My Grandma heart had already been invoked with the first two and I went into love mode. I returned to the meeting with Will in my arms and his diaper bag over my shoulder. He drew while I took notes. We made it through the day. I got the phone number from a fellow teacher who had used this woman for in home daycare with her own child. I called her, explained the situation, and how much I could afford to pay weekly. At first, she said no, but she could hear the panic in my voice and conceded to the amount and Will could start in the morning. What a blessing she was!! All I could say when I got off the phone was Thank you JESUS! Will lived with Abigail and I for 6 months. Benjamin had found a 2 bedroom apartment he could afford in a pretty decent area not far from his work. He fixed it up for Will and it looked really cute for a 2 year old. He was able to find a sitter that would come to the apartment. They were able to spend Christmas together as a mini family. Prior to Will coming to live with him, Benjamin had gone to court and gotten custody of Will with my financial help. Benjamin was so excited to have Will living with him. He made the desires of his heart known to the LORD. At some point he would like to have custody of his other two boys. The LORD listens!! Two months later in February, Michael and Adam's Mom dropped them off at Benjamin's apartment saying she had had enough of them they were all his. Benjamin warned her that she would not get them back that he would go to court and get custody. The boys had been in and out of homeless shelters with their mom. They were out of school more than they were in and as a result very far behind in their grade level skills. Their little eyes had seen more abuse both physical and emotional than anyone can imagine. I helped Benjamin out financially and paid for the attorney in order for him to legally get custody. That Grandma heart sprang into action one more time.

As I have mentioned in a previous chapter Benjamin married Maria in June of 2016. Maria had a son, David, from a previous relationship that was the same age as Adam. My Grandma hat expanded to loving 4 Grandsons. Then in April of 2017 Maria gave birth to another son, Benjamin Thomas whom I call BT. I was the proud Grandma of 5 Grandsons, all wonderful, and special to me in very different ways. The LORD has blessed me beyond measure.

In May of 2020 Michael and I welcomed our first Grand Daughter into the world and our family. Scarlett arrived on May 4, 2020 during the beginnings of COVID-19. Allyson knew her name well before she was born. She had known from a young age that if she ever had a daughter, she would name her Scarlett. She honored her mom by giving Scarlett the middle name of Leslie. This little girl is pure delight for me. She is the one that bonded Allyson and I together. I felt that I could counsel Allyson with the questions she had about motherhood. I was able to support her emotionally woman to woman friend to friend. I was able to talk to Allyson from a mother's perspective and she would listen. When Michael tried to talk to her about the same things, they butted heads. Michael and I went to Allyson and Brandon's home the week she came home from the hospital with Scarlett. We brought food for a week, and cooked Allyson 3 meals a day and warmed up meals for Brandon when he came home from the restaurant. He is the Executive Chef for Shore Raw Bar and Grill in Austin. We did laundry and cleaning for the week. I was there to encourage her through her trials of being able to nurse, keeping up with the pumping, and recording everything that the doctors wanted from her. The LORD's timing is perfect in all things. Scarlett and I are close, we were speaking the same language at one point in time. She is growing up so fast and is so smart. I don't want to miss a moment of it. Allyson is now pregnant with her second child, also a girl. They have decided on Camille for her name. This Grandma can't wait to welcome this new little one into the family March 1 (or late February) 2022. Allyson recently asked if we were going to come for a week again after she comes home with Camille. She told us it had been so helpful and she really wants us to be a part of Camille's life. Of course, we are going to be there!!

My next Grandma moment came when Michael's son Matthew and his wife, Sarah gave birth to a baby girl. Lucy Reese was born on September 28, 2020. This was our second Grand Daughter giving us a total of 7 Grandchildren!! Matt and Sarah struggled to have children and went through the process of IVF. Their first implant was lost in miscarriage. Their second implant was our precious little Lucy. It is hard to believe that she just celebrated her first birthday last month in September 2021.

Matthew and Sarah are going to try for a boy this next round of implanting. Michael and I are very excited about that prospect. Both Lucy and Scarlett are so cute together. They are only 5 months apart and definitely look related to one another almost sister like. Baby boy Beasley is doing great!! Sarah has graduated from the fertility doctor to an Obstetrician. This newest bundle of blue of Matthew and Sarah's will be close in age to Allyson's second child. GOD is good all the time, all the time GOD is good.

I love my grandma hat and I'm not ready to hang it up. These 7 soon to be 9 grandchildren are part of my life line in fighting COVID-19 and my recovery. I want to see them grow up and become the best that they can be. I want them to know the LORD and give their lives over to HIM. My Grandma hat and faith hat will be in place to share wisdom, HIS love, and the way to HIM. Thank you, JESUS, for entrusting me with this opportunity to live by example, word, and deed for these young grandchildren of mine.

I AM: *A Warrior*
(as told by my husband, daughter, and my son)

*A*s I said in my first chapter, I do not have any recollection of my fight with COVID-19 from the time I first entered the hospital in Brenham on July 10 to when I was brought out of my drug induced slumber the day before extubation and saw my entire family surrounding me. I have asked my husband, daughter, and son to share with me the timeline of my fight from each of their perspectives. Each of their experiences follows next. I will pick up my faith journey in the next chapter, I AM: A Fighter.

From my loving husband Michael:

My beautiful, wonderful wife, and best friend has asked me to write a portion of this chapter for her book from my perspective as her husband. I am not a writer like she is for sure. I do not have the details and daily timeline of events like my step daughter, Abby. My writing skills may jump between 1st person, to the reader and to Claudia. So, bear with me and soak in my attempt to inform and bring to life the events that I experienced.

To begin with I was not surprised when the test results were revealed. She had been caring for me, for 3 days with my helpless "Man-flu" as she jokingly called it. I had all the normal COVID symptoms but seemed to be coming through it with my returned taste and smell within 6 days. I was crushed emotionally when she tested positive for COVID July 8, and just 2 days later, decided she was so uncomfortable trying to catch her breath that she should get checked out at the local hospital.

I called ahead to see how they wanted to handle a COVID positive in-person examination visit to the ER. The hospital said that she could walk in get checked and they would let me know what they found. I could only watch her walk in that front door. I was starting to get worried when she was admitted to the local hospital, with COVID. I could only get updates once a day and accessing her labs online was always a day later than when she was tested. After no reports of improvement, I asked the hospital nurse if they would give her Ivermectin as a possible treatment instead of just Remdesivir. I was told that it was not "hospital protocol". They would however, give her plasma with antibodies as a second treatment. I am a fixer by nature, but I couldn't fix her, heal her, or be by her side. This is more than the average cold or Flu for her.

Since she took her phone with her, we texted a lot and even a couple of video calls. As long as these were happening and she seemed to be comfortable; I knew she was still okay, even though feeling crappy and needing a little oxygen. The hospital finally agreed to let me visit on the outside of the room window to see that she was doing okay and they were taking good care of her.

When I got to visit with her on the third day through the window, I could not hear her, her voice was so weak. I remember my visit the day before. She seemed to be feeling a little better and hopeful she had rounded the corner. Now, she looked so weak lying there in the bed, pale with a featureless face. There was no energy or spark to be able to communicate with me. I asked if she was okay and the nurse told me she was on a very high amount of oxygen through a high flow nasal cannula. I went home from that visit feeling very helpless, sad, and emotionally weak. I felt like something was not quite right. My update later that evening was the usual though. She is resting comfortably and stable. So, no bad news is good news, right?

The call at 1:45 AM on July 15 was totally unexpected and has landed us on a new course. The caller from the hospital said they had "Sedated you, put you on a ventilator, and you would be taken by Life-Flight to the hospital in College Station". I was in a state of shock and confusion as I tried to process what I had just heard. The hospital called to say, "She had taken a turn for the worse, not being able to breathe; and they had to sedate her, intubate her, put her on a ventilator, and life-flight her to the College Station hospital to be placed in the ICU." My mind started racing, "What should I do? Who should I call? If I drive up to College Station which hospital? Will they even let me see her?" LORD help me!

I knew I needed to call Abby. She is a nurse and understands vital signs, lab results and readings from the California COVID perspective. She is also listed as a power of attorney after me; in case I had a relapse or unforeseen event. It was important to me to let her know how sick her mom had become. It was a hard call to make. I remained as calm as I could and gave her the situation as I knew it.

I was talking to Abby from the College Station hospital Emergency Room parking lot; a doctor called to let me know you had arrived and would be going to ICU shortly. I asked if I could see you and he informed me that I would not be able to see you since you would be placed in COVID isolation for several days. There was nothing I could do and I should just go home and not worry. I turned around and headed back home with such a heavy heart. During my conversation with Abby, she told me she would make arrangements with her work and get a flight out as soon as she could. So, it was a long drive back home at 3:45 AM.

After I got home that early morning the silence, the quietness, in the house was overbearing. Claudia was not there; her presence was notably absent and I didn't even know if she would ever be here again. She is my best friend and we do everything together. I didn't know what I would do without her. I love her so much. I thought "This can't be happening again".

The next morning, I reached out to a member of our Life Group from church. She would text often and check up on Claudia and see how I was doing as well and if I needed anything. I kept her updated with the little I was told and she updated the rest of the group and our church family. I knew I needed a strong prayer presence after the phone call I got from the hospital. I also heard from our Pastor and was assured Claudia would be on the prayer list for the Pastors and Elders of the church. It was such a comfort to know we were being covered in prayer.

The day she was admitted, the College Station hospital's "protocol" had just been changed to "No Visitors". This presented a whole new set of challenges. The hours after hours ticked by-was there any change? Has she improved? Is she recovering? What's going on? Who is her doctor?

It was such a relief when Abby and I received word that the protocol had been changed again and now she was "out of COVID isolation" and it was okay to have a visitor. I could finally touch her, hold her hand, and tell her "I love you" and she would know she was not alone. I let Abby stay with her for the first few nights because I knew she was on a limited visitation schedule. We then decided to alternate who would visit during the day and who would get permission to stay overnight with her in ICU. We both needed an out of hospital day of rest.

The real reality and hardest day was the day I requested the Palliative Care Doctor tell us about the next steps. She was nearing 2 weeks on the ventilator and her Directive to Physician states that she did not want to be kept on a ventilator. The Palliative Care Doctor asked Abby to leave the room while the 3 of us discussed Claudia's possible outcome.

The doctor reduced her sedation medication to bring her into a semi-cognitive state of mind. He asked several questions which required yes or no nods and a thumbs up or down answer indication. He wanted to make sure Claudia was capable of making decisions for herself. He determined she could understand the situation and make these life decisions for herself. He gave us the options as he saw them; what they would entail, and also explained what it could mean for Claudia to be taken off the ventilator.

Option 1: Remove the ventilator hose and intubation apparatus from her mouth and throat. We could see if your body was able to just function on its own.

Option 2: Remove the ventilator hose and intubation apparatus from her mouth and throat. Place a bi-pap mask (with forced ventilator air). If that wasn't sufficient with just masking, he could then perform a tracheotomy and hook it back up to a ventilator. This would also require putting a feeding tube directly into her stomach. He also shared that only 1 other patient had survived coming off the ventilator and not doing the tracheotomy step

Option 3: Come off the ventilator, try the mask, but not connect it to the ventilator just supplemental oxygen.

Claudia through a series of questions indicated that she would agree to coming off the ventilator and no to the tracheotomy. Yes, to using the supplemental oxygen.

I cried, but I supported her and her decision.

We called Abby back into the room and told her of our conversation and the decision made. The doctor shared that he was not confident that Claudia would survive. He told us that we needed to contact family to have them come say their final goodbyes and to have funeral arrangements made the day before she was extubated. He then raised the sedation level which put her back into a restful sleep.

We went home and got busy contacting family to let them know what was going on and what the decision was that you had made. Many family members were shocked and not happy about the decision. This was very frustrating for me because I know what your wishes are and what is written in your living will, what was discussed between us, and what was said in the meeting with the doctor. I didn't want to lose you but I knew I had to support you and your decision.

All of the kids and their spouses, both brothers and spouses with one on video chat, and her 3 oldest Grandsons with another one on video chat came to see her. They could have some alone time with her and say what they wanted to her, love on her, spend the last few moments that they could with her. It was a long exhausting day for her for sure. After the last visitor left, I held her hand as they again administered the sedation to help her get some sleep for the big day ahead.

The following day was extubating day. Abby, Ben, and I would be there with her to pray and help with her fight to survive. I updated our Life Group and Pastor what would be happening the next day. Under "normal life conditions" our Pastor would be present to help all of us through this event. However due to "hospital COVID protocol" even the Pastors were not being allowed into the hospital. So sad! But I knew even remote prayers will cover her with blessings and would be an integral part of her recovery and healing. Needless to say, I didn't sleep well that night; and in the quiet of my bedroom I cried, I prayed, I asked for a miracle. I prayed for complete and total healing.

The day had arrived. Ben, Abby, and I were in the room with her, the doctor, and the nurses. The three of us were at the foot of her bed holding hands to give strength to one another. The doctor lowered the sedation; asked her if she was ready and she nodded yes.

The doctor had told us that if her oxygen level dropped to the 80's it would be touch and go, the 70's not much hope, and the 60's would begin transition. The transition (at 56 the lips turn purple without oxygen), then on to death; might be quick, but they would make her as comfortable as possible during the process.

My eyes were locked on that oxygen monitor. She started in the mid 90's due to the ventilator providing pure oxygen to her lungs. It wasn't long before she dropped into the 80's, then 70's. I squeezed Abby's hand hard and she squeezed back. I just kept repeating in my head "Oh LORD My GOD, YOUR Will be Done, if it is by your design". When she dropped down to the 60's Abby became more verbal. She told her mom to fight for it; she was strong. As the seconds flashed by Claudia's oxygen saturation levels started coming back up, and up, and up. It was at that point that the Doctor and nurses started fitting her with the bi-pap which she didn't like very well. We could tell she was struggling all the way, but she got back up to 92%. They made several unsuccessful attempts in fitting her with a forced oxygen mask, but she was having none of that. Finally, they located and agreed to trying just a high flow nasal cannula, similar to the one she had worn at the first hospital before going on the ventilator. It took the flow rate being cranked up to the max flow of the gauge, but that was okay with her. She was doing it on her own.

After a few days she seemed to be in pretty good spirits and was ready to go home! It was hard convincing her that she was still very weak and would need a lot of physical therapy to be able to gain strength to walk again. But she was alive and breathing on her own a true modern day miracle. Thank you, GOD!

Abby had to head back to California to go back to work. I stayed with her day and night. She seemed to need me there to keep her calm. I think she was worried about going to sleep and not waking up. They did have her on some pretty strong medications, so they were still swirling around in her system. She was not even strong enough to feed herself, so I was there to feed her all meals. The hospital had her on a very bland soft diet that was very boring. She was a trooper though and ate the best she could. The speech pathologists came to have her try eating puddings and crackers to make sure she could swallow properly and were able to change up the menu to a soft mechanical diet. She remained on that for the remainder of her stay in the College Station hospital.

After several days she was moved from ICU to a regular room. Then after only a couple of days discussions began about where she would need to go next, for rehab. Her oxygen flow needs were still too high for any of the inpatient physical therapy facilities. The hospital placement coordinator was working with me and Claudia's insurance company to find a long term location for her. Going home was not an option.

My sister, Sandra actually found a Long Term Acute Care facility in New Braunfels. Wow, it was in Claudia's network and they had an opening. I could stay with my sister at night and spend the days with her at the facility. They had a slightly different policy on that "overnight visitors protocol" thing. The hospital coordinator and I worked on getting insurance approval for this Long Term Acute Care facility and the transportation needed to get there. Claudia would be leaving on August 14, after being in the hospital since July 10, going on 36 days.

So, I will close. I will share with you that I had truly been afraid that I would never be able to sleep in the same bed, sit with Claudia on the couch and have our morning coffee while watching the news together. Share our worldly views on how things should be. I am just so grateful that GOD listens to prayers and performs miracles. She is a modern day walking talking miracle.

A letter from your daughter Abigail:

Dear Mama,

I am here to tell you a story. Just like when you used to tell me stories when I was a little girl. This story is your story of surviving COVID-19, just like how you have survived so much in this life. I am here to fill in the missing pieces of your memory; to tell you that you are a living miracle. Here is your story from the perception of a nurse trying her best to stay in the role as your daughter.

You had been in the hospital since July 10th with COVID-19. Your symptoms started around July 6 after Mike had gotten sick on July 1st. You texted me on July 8 that you both were COVID positive. I had been dealing with COVID-19 since day one in the Emergency room (ER) in a busy Level II trauma center out in California. I have seen and dealt with many innocent patients struck by this virus; this virus that does not discriminate and takes peoples' lives with a vengeance. I remember you texting me that it was difficult to breath that Saturday morning on the 10th. You were being a bit stubborn and not finding a way to get a pulse oximeter to measure your oxygen level like I told you to. I even gave examples of how you could safely buy one and not infect others. Finally, you got one, and your oxygen level was 89-90% which is automatic hospital admission. I already knew what was about to happen to you.

It was July 14, 2021. I was sitting at home trying to stay distracted. I needed to keep my mind busy since my crying all day did not do any of us any good. I had called into work that night because I was not going to be any help to my patients. My mind was only focused on you and your health. Today was not a good day for you. Mike went to see you through the window again and for our daily update he said your "sparkle" was gone and that you looked really tired. Dread and fear sunk into my heart and stayed with me all day.

It was shortly after midnight July 15, here in California when I got.... the call. The call that nobody is ever really prepared for, not even a nurse like me. With the time difference it would have been a little after two in the morning in Texas. Mike's name popped up on my phone and I answered it immediately, "Hello?". Mike with his calm Texas drawl comes in on the other side, "I don't want you to start panicking but your mom has been intubated and put on a life-flight to another hospital... I am on my way there now. It is up to you if you want to come down or not. Not sure what you have to do with work...hold on they are calling me from the hospital." I anxiously waited for Mike to return to our call with any sort of news. All I kept thinking about was "You are my only mother and I will be by your side, always". I already knew what I had to do. I started texting my managers about what was happening and I was planning to buy a ticket home. "Okay I'm back", I hear Mike's voice again, "She has made it to the ER and she is still intubated. They are redrawing her labs; she is stable and should be going to the ICU in a bit. They won't let me or anyone in since she has COVID. So, I am heading home. Have you made a decision on what you want to do?" I tell him, "I will be there the first flight I can get. I only have one mother and she needs me right now." Little did I know how much you were going to really need me. I told Mike I will be looking at flights first thing in the morning. I needed to get things ready on my end and I would let him know my flight information so he could pick me up. Then we hung up.

As soon as we got off the phone, I immediately started to weep like I had never wept before. Soon I felt a furry little paw wipe at my wet cheeks and then the unexpected rough tongue licking up my salty tears. Francesca, my new kitten was trying to comfort me. You did not know about my sweet little black fur ball that I had gotten just a couple weeks before. Pets were a distraction and expensive in your eyes for my life but I got her anyway. In the moment of her being able to calm me down I heard the word "pray" in my heart. I immediately went down onto my knees and started to pray. I had not prayed in a long time, to be honest; especially on my knees. I knew this could not be how your story ended. You have overcome so much in your life: survivor of three abusive marriages, enduring multiple miscarriages, single mother of two children that had their own life challenges you had to support, surviving sexual assault and PTSD that comes along with it. These last ten years have been the happiest years of your life when Mike came into our lives. You deserved so much more time with him and the happy life you have created together. I prayed for GOD's healing mercy to be over you, to guide the medical staff taking care of you, praising HIM for all the things HE has helped you overcome and what HE will be doing for you in your life once you are healed. Then I heard in my heart "Get up."

My hands were shaking. I called Adrian, the only boyfriend you have ever approved, to come over to be with me. I did not want to be alone in that moment. I was frantic and I needed him to be my calmness. He has always been the Ying to my Yang. I told him what happened and he immediately hugged me and I wept in his arms until it was time to head to the airport. He dropped me off and I was on my way home to you. Being in public made me have to stop crying and get into survival mode. But I felt different this time in the airport. Everyone was doing what they needed to do, heading to the Starbucks for a quick coffee, others running to their gates. Everything was just moving around me but time felt like it had stopped. I could not get back to Texas fast enough. Finally, I got onto my plane and was hoping to catch a nap since I had been up for 24 hours. The snacks are being passed out and I realize I still had not taken a nap. My mind will not stop thinking about you being all alone in the ICU and none of us can hold your hand. I start to get angry at COVID. I start to think why my family, why my mother? Then I start to think this is what it must feel like to be the families that have had a loved one affected by COVID-19. I have been on the nursing side of COVID and had empathy for the families and patients. Now I start to have sympathy since COVID has now affected my family personally. I begin to humble myself. I decided to try to eat the snacks that were handed to me earlier. I start to eat the sweet caramel waffle cookie and felt a huge crunch in my mouth. Part of my crown came off. This was definitely not my day.

It is still July 15. Touchdown; finally, I am in Texas, my home sweet home! Mike picks me up and we drove by the hospital you were staying at. I knew you could not see me or hear me, I still told you I was here and I loved you as we passed by. Then I said a little prayer for you. It was important for my peace of mind that you felt you were not alone, no matter what the outcome was going to be. It was difficult not being able to be by your side to hold you and tell you I love you. Being a nurse, I understood why we could not see you. Policies meant nothing to me as a daughter that needed to be with her mother. I even brought a new N95 mask I am fitted for at work to see if I could get special approval from the hospital supervisor to see you. I wanted any time I could get with you, especially since I was not sure how long work was going to allow me to stay. Mike said he was waiting for an update on your status for the day. So, we headed to the previous hospital you were at to pick up the rest of your belongings that were left behind. Then we went home.

I went upstairs to set my things down in the guest room. Your glasses were sitting on the nightstand and the quietness surrounded me. I missed feeling your energy around me. You knew how to light up a room. I missed talking to you, hearing your obnoxious laugh, getting my mama bear hugs. You have been my rock, my biggest supporter, my best friend, and the most important person in my life. Your voice, your laugh, your touch was nowhere to be heard or felt. I saw the digital photo slide show frame sweeping pictures across the screen. There were pictures of your beautiful smile and your eyes full of life and joy. Yearning for you overtook me and I started to cry. Mike's voice started to rumble upstairs calling my name to come down for dinner. I wiped my tears because I knew I had to be strong for him too.

It was evening time and we still had not gotten a call about your status. I looked at the clock and saw it was seven at night. I knew shift change was happening and it would be difficult to get a nurse on the phone at that time. So, Mike and I waited patiently until 07:45 PM; I even gave them an extra 15 minutes. We finally got a hold of the nurse taking care of you 20 minutes later. She gave us the labs I asked for since I had been following your results since you went into the hospital. There were a few abnormal blood tests I asked her to follow up on with the doctor. I could hear in the nurse's voice she was getting exhausted from all of my questions and her shift had just started. Luckily, I understood the feeling of burnout from this pandemic so I was able to brush her tone off. She did not have time to set up the video chat system they have for patients unable to have visitors. We had to just trust that you were "stable and comfortable".

That was the phrase that we kept getting anytime we would call for updates. It would take a while to get nurses on the phone and be able to have time to talk to them; but we needed more than "stable and comfortable". None of the nurses could get the video chat system to work which added to the frustration of being stuck at home away from you. I was denied visitation to see you since you were still on isolation. No VIP treatment for us, our family was just like all the other families affected by COVID; nurse's family or not. Mike and I needed answers that we could see and understand so we decided to take things into our own hands. You know we both like to problem solve and fix things. I mean I take care of people for a living; this is right up my ally.

The next day Mike gave me your login information to your health portal that you had been getting the updates from while in the hospital. Username and password entered. Then your name and birthday flashed across my phone screen. We were in!! Mike was your acting first medical power of attorney and you had me listed as your secondary. We felt justified to commit a federal crime against HIPPA. Mike was anxiously looking over my shoulder reading the test results as if he knew what they all meant. Luckily, I was here to help translate everything. What was in your chart was not at all the picture the nurses were presenting to us. You had multiple critical lab values that had not been followed up with, your chest x-ray was not looking good, and you needed high settings to help you breathe on the ventilator. The doctors also wrote "critical prognosis" and "prognosis poor" in multiple notes. Mike started to get very upset and was pacing the room. He started to raise his voice and speak unspeakable words that I had not heard Mike ever use before. I had never seen him this upset out of the ten years I have known him. He was about to march down to the hospital and demand the doctors to give him answers. I told him that would not help anyone and you would not want to see him this upset. The doctors' notes continued to get worse. They said that they had spoken to us in depth about your condition and prognosis and that we wanted full treatment done. We had not heard from a doctor since that 2 AM phone call saying you were intubated, put on a life-flight, and going to the Intensive Care Unit (ICU). We knew we were going against your wishes. You never wanted a machine to keep you alive. However, Mike and I knew that the machine was just helping you heal, so to us we had justifications. If it came to the point where it was only a machine keeping you existing, we would call it and let you pass. This is why we were listed as your medical power of attorneys.

Mike immediately got on the phone and assertively asked for the charge nurse. He informed her that we would like an update from a doctor; that you had been in the ICU for 2 days and we had not heard from a doctor since you were in their ER. He also informed them that we saw the doctor's notes saying that they had spoken to us in depth, which was not true at all. One of your doctors even wrote names of whom he spoke to and let me tell you they were not our names. A male voice came over the phone. It was the doctor...finally! He kept trying to tell us he was sorry, he thought that he had spoken to us and that he has a very busy ICU with 17 intubated patients and all of their families are constantly calling for updates. I told him I understood since I work in a busy level II trauma center. However, some of his actions and in-actions, were unacceptable. I asked the doctor if he had followed up with the critical lab values I saw in your chart from when you were in the ER. He had not and was adding the test to be redrawn to compare. The doctor agreed with me that these tests should have been followed up with and depending on what the new results showed would determine what his next steps would be. He went over the labs and x-ray he had for that day. Your health portal would post the information 24 hours later so I was limited to your current status. We discussed that we wanted to have a Do Not Resuscitate (DNR) placed on you which included no chest compressions and no shocking if your heart stopped or went into an abnormal heart rhythm. As a nurse I know with your age and condition you were in, doing everything medically possible to keep you alive would just be torture to your body and soul. Mike and I agreed to keep you comfortable but we were still in healing mode. That is all Mike kept saying for the 13 days you were on the ventilator..." We are still in healing mode."

About an hour after we got off the phone with the doctor the phone rang again. Mike said it was the hospital and we both looked at each other nervously. The doctor asked to speak to me since talking in the medical terminology was comfortable for him and he knew I would understand what he was saying. There was relatively good news but a lot of bad news followed. One of your critical lab values that was sensitive to blood clots was improving, still elevated but improving. He promised to continue to monitor this. Any little good news we took and held on to it as tight as we could for any sense of hope. Now the not so good news... the other critical lab value I asked for them to run was elevated. It was a way for them to determine if you were in Acute Respiratory Distress Syndrome or ARDS, which causes an inflammatory response and fluid buildup in the lungs and body. Normal is less than 10, to see if you needed a special medication to help prevent you from going into ARDS is given when it is 80 or above. You were 98, so you were given this medication along with aggressive steroids, antibiotics, sedatives to keep you from pulling your tubes and wires, pain medication, diuretics to help get rid of the extra fluid buildup, and blood thinners. They were able to give you your regular medications and nutrition through the feeding tube that was inserted through your nose into your stomach called a nasal-gastric tube or NG tube. The doctor was also calling back because your vital signs were starting to take a turn for the worse. Your blood pressure was dropping from all of the medications you needed and being sick in general. They already started to prone you. Studies had shown laying COVID patients with

ARDS on their bellies, or proning, had better outcomes. However, COVID patients with ARDS have a very low survival rate. The doctor was trying to do everything he could to help you survive this. He said to us, "I want to throw everything at her except for the kitchen sink.", since you were now a DNR.

We had to make the decision to start a central line to start a medication that would help bring your blood pressure to a more stable level. However, this medication is harmful to IV catheters inserted in the arms/legs. It would need to be placed in a larger vein, either groin or neck area. This is called a central line. When your blood pressure is dropping you risk not getting good oxygenated blood to your brain and other vital organs. For you to survive this and still function normally, we needed your blood pressure to be stable. Mike and I agreed it was okay for the doctor to do this. As Mike said again, "It is for her healing."

A couple hours later the doctor called us back to inform us you were "comfortable and stable". Mike started working in the garage to stay busy. I went on a walk to clear my head, to meditate, and to pray. On this walk I started to have some negative thoughts about what was going to happen to you. I had caught Mike a couple of times talking about you in the past tense. I would correct him immediately and make sure he changed his statements to speak about you in the present tense. I could only imagine what he was thinking and feeling. He lost his first wife through medical issues and then he found love again through you. He must have felt like he was losing you too. Hearing that negative thought process had me starting to think, "What if all of my praying does not work, again, and you do die?" The last time I had prayed and begged GOD to help me with my trauma, HE did not answer my prayers; at least in the way I thought HE should have. I realized this later in my life journey. This was during an experience in my life where I felt like I needed justice and HE did not answer my prayer for that. That was why I had not prayed in such a long time. Once again, I heard a word in my heart "mustard seed". I remember passages in the Bible that talk about having Faith as big as a mustard seed and GOD will follow through on HIS promises. I knew we had a huge prayer chain going for you; people all over Texas, California, Nebraska, New Mexico and even up to Canada. The Bible also says that GOD hears prayers when two or more come together to pray. I started to cry and ask GOD to forgive my negative thoughts, for not trusting HIM, for only coming to HIM when I needed HIM. I confessed that I knew that was not how this relationship is meant to be. I prayed for HIM to hear all the prayers that were about you and to follow through with these prayers as HE has promised. That I will give HIM my trust, control, fears, and have faith even if it is only as big as a mustard seed.

We were told that we should be able to use the video chat system they have set up for patients on isolation the next day. I called Ben to tell him to come over so we could do the video chat as a family. You could hear our voices and know we were praying and thinking about you. I also am trained to look at a person and see how stable or unstable they are. I wanted to see how truly "comfortable and stable" you were. After I got off the phone with Ben, Mike and I sat down to dinner. It was very quiet other than the scraping of the metal from our utensils onto the glass plates. The house did not feel the same with you gone. It was too quiet, too empty. I saw the calendar in the corner of my eye. I saw what today's date was, July 16th. This is yours and Mike's wedding anniversary. Mike finally broke the silence. He looks up from his plate and I see the sadness in his eyes when he said "I do everything with your mom. She's my best friend. I don't know what I'm going to do without her." I had no words I could give him to take away the pain he was feeling. All I could do was be there in the silence with him, I reached out and held his hand.

Saturday rolled around. You had been on the ventilator for going on three days now. Ben made it over in the morning. We were trying to be patient and wait for our daily update, which seemed to happen around 1 PM. We all tried to make small talk until our patience was running thin waiting for a call. It was going on 4 PM and Ben needed to start heading home. But he was promised a video call with you and that was what we were going to get. The nurses were trying their best to get the system to work but they could not get it to go past the hospital's firewalls. GOD was looking out for us and knew we needed to see you for a glimpse of hope. A random nurse that was not even on your service heard about us trying for multiple days to do the video chat system and had been unsuccessful. She took out her personal phone and allowed us to use face time to see you and talk to you. We kept it short out of respect of her still needing to take care of her actual patients. She was an angel in our eyes. Mike, like always, stayed strong when talking to you. He told you he missed and loved you and he could not wait to have you sitting next to him on the couch watching the news and drinking coffee together. Ben did his best to try and hold it together. He got out the most important things to him: he loved you, that he and his friends were praying for you, and that you were not alone. As the boys were saying what they needed to say I was going into nurse mode. I was observing how swollen you appeared. I saw some abrasions on your neck that I wanted answers about, I was monitoring the vital sign machine and looking at the ventilator settings. I am trained to put pieces together of a puzzle, to solve a problem, to fix things and make them better. I am usually the one at the bedside doing the adjustments of the medications, suctioning, turning, cleaning, figuring out the labs and what they mean and how to correct them etc. I now understood the doctors' comments "condition: critical" and "poor prognosis". You were sick! I made sure to tell you I loved you and repeated what

Ben said, that you were not alone. As soon as we can see you, we will.

The next week we tried to stay busy. We had to wait 20 days from the initial start of your symptoms before they would take you off isolation to be able to have visitors. I never got approved by the hospital supervisor to come visit you. Luckily work was very understanding of the situation and told me to take all the time I needed, that family comes first. Anytime the phone rang we would jump up from where we were and run to the phone to check if it was the hospital or not. The unknowing of what was happening to you and not being by your side was the most difficult part about the whole situation. It was frustrating and even infuriating at times, scary, and feelings of being helpless being away from you. Mike let me borrow your robe at the house so I could smell your perfume on it. I slept with it every night and I used it as my blanket when watching TV on the couch downstairs with Mike. This did give me some comfort and I appreciated him for thinking about me and doing that.

Isolation was finally lifted on July 24 and we could come see you. I had not been sleeping very well, but the night before we could see you, I was able to rest. Knowing I could finally see you, gave me comfort and peace, so my mind was able to relax. The day we came to visit, you were actually awake. This was a surprise to us because we were told your ventilator settings were still too high to do the "sedation holiday" which is where they reduce the sedation that helps keep you asleep while you are on the ventilator. They do this to see how you can tolerate being at a lower setting on the ventilator to hopefully take the tracheal tube out. It was so good to see that you were still in there.... your soul was still in your body; that you were in healing mode and not just existing on a machine. Your arms, hands, and legs were so swollen. They had to remove all of your rings due to how swollen you got. The abrasion on your chin was healing well. I later found out it was a sheer injury from the sheets when they had you in the prone position, on your stomach. You were able to answer yes and no questions. It was satisfying to finally be able to have some sort of communication with you, that you saw and felt us present, and you were able to respond back to us. The hospital allowed me to stay the night with you and I did not leave your side after that until I knew you were out of the woods.

It was day 12 of being on the ventilator; it was Monday July 26th. We needed to make a decision on what the next step was going to be. As a family we had been discussing next steps but Mike and I already knew what we would do for you in respect to your wishes you have expressed to us in the past and with your living will. Most COVID patients that are not able to get off the ventilator after 14 days usually have to get a trach tube put into their neck and connected to the ventilator until they can come off, if they even do come off because some do not unfortunately. They would also place a feeding tube directly into your stomach, so you could continue to receive nutrition, if you went the trach route. The doctors and the whole family were pushing for this option. It was starting to get Mike upset, understandably, and I felt like I was in the middle trying to keep everyone at peace. I had been updating family and friends on your status the whole time you were hospitalized. Mike and I knew you did not want to just exist on a machine. There was no guarantee that you would be able to get off the trach ventilator if we went this route. We knew we could not do this route to keep you here existing on a machine for our own selfishness. The doctors had the sedation reduced when discussing next steps with you and Mike. They asked me to step outside of the room until the conversation was finished. When I came back, I saw Mike's eyes were all red. They told me you decided you wanted them to pull the intubation tube and get off the ventilator. The doctor told us he only had one other person survive this when pulling the tube early. They said we needed to call family to say our goodbyes, and to start getting your funeral arrangements ready. They would make sure you would be comfortable during the transition. We told you that we supported your decision. I contacted the family to have them make arrangements to come see you one last time before we pulled the tube. I updated your friends as well and they started to pray even harder for you.

It was the next day and everyone was trying to come say their goodbyes to you. The security downstairs was not informed on what was happening to you and why so many people were trying to come see you. There was a new policy that only one person could come visit per day. They were not letting anyone up until they had a manager explain the situation to them. Mike and I had to make a list of everyone that was planning to see you so they could check them in. Once everyone was allowed in, we stayed out in the waiting room and would only have 1-3 people in your hospital room at a time to say their last words to you. I stayed in the waiting room until everyone had left. I had been by your side 24 hours a day once we were allowed to visit you. I knew I needed to allow you your time with the rest of the family and allow the family to have their intimate alone moments with you. Both of your brothers, Mark and Stephen came. Unfortunately, Aunt Virginia was not able to make it but was able to be there through video chat. Aunt Kristin was able to make it. Even through the sadness of the day she was still able to help bring smiles to everyone's faces with her gift of humor. Both of your step-children, Matt and Allyson were able to come see you along with their spouses. I know how close you have gotten to Mike's kids and how much they love you and appreciate you in Mike's life. Ben and his biological three older boys came to see you; while David, his step-son was on video chat when they were in the room saying what they wanted to say to their favorite grandma. Benjamin Jr. was just too little to understand or see you all hooked up to wires and tubes everywhere, so he did not get to see you. I know how much you love your grandchildren and how you have sacrificed to help these boys have a good life with their dad, your son, full time.

It was a long day but everyone got their time with you. When I went into the room you looked exhausted. I asked you if you wanted me to ask the nurse to increase your sedation for you to rest. You had a big day with everyone and an even bigger day to prepare for tomorrow. You nodded your head yes. As the medicine dripped into your veins faster your eyelids became heavy and you fell asleep. Eventually I made it over to the hospital couch and closed my eyes for some rest as well.

It was close to midnight and something told me to wake up. This had happened a few other nights when I was staying in your hospital room. Every time that feeling surged through me, I would wake up to see you wide awake. I would play some music for you, pray over you, tell you that you are a survivor, and the strongest person I know. I would tell you to keep fighting while rubbing your forehead or holding your hand. You would fall back to sleep when I would do this and I would continue to tell you these important facts. This time was no different when I opened my eyes, I saw you wide awake just looking around the room. I went over to your side and started to begin my yes/no questions to try and communicate with you. I wanted to know what you were feeling and thinking. You looked like you had

1,000 thoughts racing through your mind. You shook your head "no" when I asked you if you were scared or anxious. I asked you "Are you upset with Mike and me that we allowed you to be and stay intubated?" You shook your head "no". Next, I asked "Are you glad to be alive?" and you nodded "yes". I asked you if you wanted to die and you shook your head "no". After I saw that answer I started to ask you multiple questions about things you would be willing to try to help you survive once the tube is out. We made a list together and I wrote it down on the white board in the room to show the doctor the next day before turning off the ventilator of what you were willing to try. Your version of "throw everything at it except for the kitchen sink."

I wanted you to get your rest so I asked the nurse to increase your sedation more; you did say you were starting to be in pain. I wanted you to be comfortable and rested. They maxed you out on the medications they were using to help with pain and sedation. You were still awake. So, I decided to talk to you and keep you company. I talked about work, Adrian, California, and missing home. You wanted me to tell you what happened to you and how you got to where you were that day; when I asked if you wanted to hear the story of course I shared with you. So, I broke down the details to you and your eyes would get really big at certain parts. I asked you if you remembered any of it and you said no. Since you were on sedation medication when I told you what happened, it makes sense why you do not remember this now. I tried to make light of the situation and talk about how you have a feeding tube in your nose and that the nutrition they are giving you looks like a big bag full of vanilla milkshake. That Ben joked to one of the nurses that they need to switch it to Strawberry flavor because "you are a strawberry girl". You tried to laugh but then a coughing spell happened. The nurses came in to suction you and eventually your oxygen levels came back up and you were not struggling anymore. Once I saw you were comfortable again, I thought this was a good time to bring up Francesca to you. I remember joking with Ben on the phone about how I was going to tell you. That at least I'm telling you while you were intubated and on drugs so you could not lecture me about getting a pet. Luckily you took me telling you about Francesca well and you even nodded yes that you thought she was cute. You were glad I had someone to come home to and keep me company. You were happy I got her. It could have also been the drugs talking. Finally, around 5:30 AM you started to doze back to sleep and once I saw you were asleep, I was able to shut my eyes too.

I woke up and saw Mike holding your hand and talking to you about the everyday things happening outside of the hospital. It was so wonderful to see him so attentive to you. The last few days when he would come to visit, he would stand by the window and stare out of it instead of holding your hand and talking to you. When you wanted Mike, we had to tell him to go hold your hand because you only wanted him. He is your person.

It was upsetting as a daughter to not see him as attentive as he normally is with you. Luckily, I was understanding of his behavior because of what Mike had been through with the loss of his previous wife; which must have brought up old feelings and memories. So, it was delightful to see him supporting you on such a big day and working through his emotions. They were not letting Ben in since the hospital had changed their policy with visitation. So once again we had to have the management explain to security to let him in since the doctor did not think you would survive extubating the breathing tube. As a patient and family, we had the right to be with you during your possible transition. The hospital respected this and was advocating for us to be with you. Eventually Ben made his way up to the room.

Once Ben and the staff were in the room, we discussed our white board plan together. I remember hearing Ben say to the doctor, "You don't know my mama! She is a tough woman and she's been through a lot; she can get through this. She's going to be patient number two!" With that the doctor had the team start the extubating process while we prayed. You were nodding your head yes, hard, when he asked if you were ready! I have always seen the breathing tube being placed but never removed. We were told by the nurse the day before we would be in another room when it happened but we were all there standing at the foot of your bed hand in hand, Mike on my left and Ben to my right. As quick as the tube goes in, it was quick to be removed. We were told that if your oxygen gets down into the 70's or lower it would be quick for you to transition. You were at 90% and then started to drop in the 80's Ben started to grab my hand harder. Then 70's and my left hand got squeezed by Mike's hand. You were coughing and it looked like you were losing all of your oxygen rather than getting any oxygen into you. We were all saying our own little prayers during this moment. My prayer was simply, "LORD breathe air of life into her lungs… breathe air of life into her lungs…" You were struggling to breathe and going into distress. As a nurse I wanted to step in and be a part of the team to get you better, I needed to have you better. I was glad Mike and Ben were there holding my hands, like they were keeping me grounded in that spot; I needed to be the daughter and not the nurse.

The respiratory therapists were moving as fast as they could and of course in that moment it didn't feel fast enough when you dropped down to 68%. Then I grabbed Mike and Ben's hands even harder. Eventually the numbers on the monitor started to go up to the 70's, 80's…90's, 94%. I will take anything above 92% (bare minimum level the body needs to have to function properly). They had to try on a few different masks for the Bi Pap machine they put you on. This simply works similarly to a ventilator just not as invasive. But many patients, including you, do not tolerate this machine because the masks can feel "claustrophobic" from what I've been told by my patients and their families. You wore it for a couple of hours but were ready to leave! You were a bit goofy from the drugs they had you on. You could only whisper and it was hard to hear with the mask over your face. You tried to use your own "sign language" to communicate with us when we could not understand your whispers. You first placed your index and middle finger pointing downward like two legs and stared to move them as if your fingers were walking in the air. We asked if you wanted to leave? You said yes, we all started to laugh and told you not yet but that you will go home when you get better. Your face looked so confused, "Like better? I am better, got the tube out let's go!" Your legs were like wet noodles. You had been lying in bed for 19 days.

There were a few other goofy things from that first day when you had the tube removed. You kept pointing to the clock and your arm where you would normally wear your watch, but your arm was too swollen to wear it. We told you that you needed to wear the Bi Pap mask for at least two hours, hoping you would get adjusted to it and let it help you heal. You kept watch on the clock and you started to count down to when you can take it off. Down to the seconds you put your hands up and counted down 10,9, 8...3,2,1. Mask was off and they put you back on the high flow nasal cannula that was heated/humidified. This is what you were wearing before they had to place the breathing tube into your lungs. This made you more comfortable. You looked tired and you would take little cat naps and wake back up with a shocked look on your face. We were not sure what you were feeling or thinking until you explained yourself. Now I understand it was the medications they had you on for your pain and anxiety. You looked right at me while I was sitting on the little couch in your hospital room. You asked me to come closer to you. I placed my ear near your lips and you whisper "Abby, what should I dream about?" I instantly chuckled because I was not expecting this type of question. I remember telling you "Anything you want to dream about, as long as it is something positive." You closed your eyes and I could see your eyes moving underneath your closed eyelids. You open your eyes again and shake your head no. You said you could not go to sleep due to the cars racing by you. Then you kept talking about having to go to another room, which never made sense, like wanting to go lay down in the waiting room. You stayed confused like this while in the ICU but as soon as they moved you to the step down unit about two days later you were back. Weak but you were back.

Mike had been staying with you a few nights when Adrian flew down to surprise me. I had been in Texas for about three weeks and he wanted to come support me and our family. I saw you were becoming more stable and they were beginning to talk about rehab facilities with you. I asked to stay with you my last couple of days before needing to return back to California to work since I did not qualify for FMLA (Family Medical Leave Act). One night, before I had left Texas, you called me over to the bed and you looked exhausted. You told me "Abby you need to just let me go. You, Mike, and Ben need to just let me go on. I'm ready to go." Tears swelled in my eyes. I did not understand why you would say these things. At first, I took it like you wanted me to help assist you to end things but now I see you wanted us to emotionally let you go so you could pass on because you were exhausted. I started to pray over you and tell you how strong you were. You slowly started to close your eyes again. I remember telling you the next morning, "If the good LORD wants to breathe life into you then you have to just roll with that day and the next and the next. You still have a purpose."

You kept getting stronger each and every day. The nurses that took care of you would stop by your room to check on how well you were doing. All the staff were amazed at your progress. Eventually I went back to California and got my daily updates from Mike and Ben. We would try to video chat for a couple minutes if you had the energy for it. Mike and the doctors worked really hard to find a good rehab for you to go to. With the help of Mike's sister, Sandra, we were able to get you into a rehab place near her home. I came down to visit the day of your transfer August 14th. The rehab place was intense. They were going to work you! They were there to help you get your strength and endurance back. That way you can do the simple things in life that we all take for granted such as feeding yourself, brushing your teeth, standing up, etc.

Eventually you got too strong for the Long Term Acute Care or LTAC section you were in but not healthy enough to go to the other part of their rehab section there. Your insurance wanted to send you to a skilled nursing facility, which is not what you deserved. Mike worked very hard with the insurance company to get home health and oxygen set up at the house. Finally on September 8, you made it home and have been home ever since. Throughout this experience I see how important having an advocate is in these situations. Also making sure your final wishes are shared with your family so there are no difficult decisions or hard discussions after the fact. The most important part of this experience is seeing GOD hold you in HIS hands, to give you strength, and to heal you through all of this. This experience has made me humble and grateful for all HE has done and will continue to do.

Every time I come to visit you; I am amazed at how strong you get. You went from 6L oxygen when you first got home to now working on no oxygen at rest and 2-3L of oxygen when walking around. You are able to do your daily routine and you are starting to get back to your baseline health prior to COVID-19. You are continuing to work on your goal of being oxygen free for all activities by the end of 2021 and with GOD's help you can and will accomplish this goal. I am so thankful to be able to have you present in my life and those closest to you. All the praise and glory be to GOD!

I love you all the way to the moon and back!

Love from your daughter,
Abigail
XOXO

A message from your son, Benjamin:

The last time I spoke to my mom was when she was in her local hospital. Her last words to me were, "I have to go, the doctor just came in." The next update I got was that mom had been intubated and flown by helicopter life-flight to a hospital in College Station. At that time, I knew this was a serious case of COVID-19. I went out to my truck away from everyone and cried. I prayed that GOD would heal her and help her get better. I told HIM that it is not her time and that she has too much life to live for. I told GOD that I need my mom and I am not ready to let go of her.

The month of July was a very scary and sad time for all of us. We all handled the situation in our own way. I waited anxiously for the daily update from my sister, Abby or Mike. We took all the lab reports on Mom's chart and pulled any good information or positive trends to give us our daily dose of hope. As the days went by that she was in the ICU and intubated, I felt so helpless and powerless. I couldn't do anything to help.

I cried almost daily. I listened to the last voicemail that Mom left, singing me Happy Birthday, and telling me "I love you, you old man!" I played it on repeat and still have her message saved to this day.

After the period of isolation, we were finally able to go see Mom in person at the hospital. Walking into that room and seeing my mother laying there in that bed immediately brought tears to my eyes. I have never in my life seen my mother in the condition that she was in. I held her hand and sat with her for hours as did Mike and Abby. We tried to comfort Mom and each other and kept things as positive as possible just in case she could hear us. It was touch and go for a while. I started a prayer chain with people from work, my church, my pastor and friend Colin, and my friends. Mom had thousands of people praying for her recovery from Texas to Canada, to Washington and California.

The day before the scheduled extubation, the entire family came to say their words of comfort and love to Mom. There was a possibility that she would not make it off the ventilator. She made the decision to remove the tube and was at peace with what ever happened. I brought my older children, her grandchildren to say their last words and possibly goodbyes. I tried to stay strong on the outside for Mom as I told her that I love her and what she means to me. But on the inside, I was a complete wreck. When we got home, I went into the garage and just broke down, on my knees pleading with GOD to help her make it. It was just uncontrollable anguish, pain, and sorrow that I have never felt before in my life. My family and some friends were in the house and came out to hug and comfort me. We prayed together for her healing and after a while I was able to calm down.

On the day of extubation, the entire drive to the hospital I prayed. When we were all in the room and Mom was awake enough to proceed, they pulled the tube out. I was so nervous and scared. Mike, Abby, and I all held hands and held our breaths as we watched Mom take her first breaths off the ventilator. We watched the monitors and her chest rise and fall for a good while. The first couple of hours were so stressful. I was panicky and afraid that the ventilator and the disease may have damaged her lungs. We kept encouraging her and stayed by her side, reminding her of how strong of a person she is. After a few hours, Mom was switched from the Bi-Pap machine to a High-Flow cannula for her oxygen needs. This was when I was able to relax a little bit and see that she was progressing positively. I thanked GOD for answering our prayers and bringing Mom back to us.

My Mom is my best friend. She is my source for advice, comfort, and love. I talk with her several times a week about everything. When something happens in my life, she is the first person I think of to call. I may not like what she has to say when she gives advice, but I know it comes from a place of love and wanting the best for me. I missed those phone calls and talking with her.

I would be on the way home from work, and I would reach for my phone to call her and I would realize that I couldn't. Not being able to speak with her or be there in person, regardless if she could hear me or not was the hardest part about this disease. I now enjoy our multiple weekly phone calls and visits again. I love hearing my mom's voice and enjoying her warm embraces full of strength and love.

During my mother's recovery, we were all there to encourage and support her in every way she needed. I prayed and thanked HIM for every little increment of improvement in her recovery. From the lowering of the amount of oxygen she needed to being able to sit up on the bed. From taking her first steps in over a month to being almost completely free of needing oxygen. Praise GOD and GLORY be to HIM, my mother is getting stronger every day and closer to being where she was health wise before COVID-19.

For those of you who are reading this, cherish your mother. Cherish your loved ones. We are all here for only a short time on this Earth; treat your loved ones as if it may be the last moment you have with them. I know I do. I cherish you, Mom. With all my heart, I love you!

I AM: *A Fighter*

$\mathcal{L}$et me start this chapter by saying that I was on some very heavy-duty drugs to keep me sedated while on the ventilator so I wouldn't fight the intubation. I was having a dream as I was being brought out of my sedation to greet my family the day before extubation. Let me remind you here before I continue that I had no idea I was on a ventilator and I didn't know I had been put on a life-flight helicopter to another hospital.

My dream began with my daughter, Abigail, and I being taken away by some bad people and we didn't want to go with them. She had smuggled a gun on board the blimp-like plane (yes, like the Goodyear blimp). She was wounded in a struggle with one of the female flight attendants, but kept coming toward me where I was sitting on a couch. Abigail kept saying; "You can do this; You are strong; You are a fighter." She finally reached me and gave me the gun. My mother tiger came out in me ,and I started shooting the flight attendants, and shot holes into the flying blimp. We started falling from the sky; I knew we would perish, but Abigail and I would be together.

I awoke from that dream to seeing a beach scene on a huge movie screen (which was the TV screen in the ICU) in front of me. It said "Hello, Claudia." and my family started saying things like "You're back; You look great; You're our hero." I was very confused. It felt like I was on a movie set, that I had been in a dangerous movie and survived. It seemed like a celebration or party atmosphere. I heard Michael's voice and reached for his hand immediately. I never let go of that hand. I saw a man that had been in the "movie" (my dream) as a bad flight attendant. He started checking something up by my head and was out of my field of vision. I heard the voice of a female flight attendant laughing with Abigail in the background. This seemed very crazy, and I was confused by the whole experience. I felt so tired after each family member had come close to tell me they loved me, they were praying for me, thanking me for all of my support in their lives and; it was now their turn to support me. All of this totally wore me out. I was asked if I was tired; and ready to take a nap. I nodded and soon I was asleep again, still holding Michael's hand.

The next thing I remember is coming to after the extubation and a mask being put on my face to help me breathe. Michael told me it was a bi pap. I didn't like it at all because they couldn't get a good seal and it felt claustrophobic. I kept waving my hand to take it off. They tried a second mask of some kind and again I shook my head no. The next thing they tried was a heated cannula which felt very weird on my face. I remember it felt like a toy warm rubber snake. Finally, we ended up with a high flow oxygen cannula which I continue to use today. Michael and Abigail were with me throughout this whole process. I couldn't seem to speak above a whisper so they spoke for me as my advocates.

I woke up the next morning on my own. I still had residual effects of the strong drugs while I slept. My mind raced, literally, every night. I had visions of Mario like cars racing on curving twisting turning tracks, jumping tracks all at high speeds. It seemed like a video game that you bought with a credit card and I was afraid someone was going to rack up charges on my credit card. When the cars would jump tracks, I was concerned that other people would have credit card charges. Crazy I know. I even asked my daughter one night what I should dream about. She was at a loss for an answer. She told me, "Anything you want to dream about Mom as long as it is positive."

After that conversation I think the LORD heard my question. HE calmed my mind and put my concerns to rest. After I first was extubated I was afraid to go to sleep because I didn't know if I would wake up again, would I continue to breathe through the night, would my mind race again? GOD had me in HIS hands even though I had not been praying during these days in the hospital. HIS plan for me and my life were in process and HE continued to guide me in my recovery, working on healing as I slept.

I envisioned the poem "Footprints in the Sand" a picture of 2 sets of footprints mine and the LORD's footprints in the sand next to mine. When I looked back throughout my life there were many times only one set of footprints could be seen. As the poem says when only one set is visible, they are the LORD's because HE loves me and will never leave me, HE is carrying me through my trials and suffering. I love this poem and the visual that it creates. I have been able to look back on my life using 20/20 vision and I have seen where this has happened many times in my life.

The struggle and fight were real from the end of July to mid-August. I could not feed myself or get out of bed. I had a Foley catheter for urinary functions but was never put on a bedpan for bowel movements. I had to be cleaned often which was an embarrassment for a woman of my age. I felt pretty helpless. Abigail had to go back home to California to work so the daily care and feeding fell to Michael. COVID-19 protocols seemed to change daily. He had to get special permission to stay with me all day and overnight. I am so blessed to have had him there with me. I was finally able to be moved out of ICU into a regular room sometime during the first week of August.

During this transition time the hospital started working with my insurance company about the next placement. There was not much more that a hospital setting could do to improve my situation. I was still using too much oxygen to be able to go to an inpatient physical therapy facility. I was still sitting at 12-15 liters of oxygen a minute with the fast flow cannula. Many of the facilities listed on my insurance had closed or were no longer accepting patients. It was very frustrating for Michael. He only had his phone internet to work with. The in network facilities needed to be updated on the insurance website. One of the facilities my insurance wanted to send me to was in Pennsylvania where once again I would be alone with no family nearby. Michael told the insurance company they needed to update their network list and help look for a place close to Brenham so I could be near family for support during the recovery period. The hospital along with Michael had to fight to get approval for a Long Term Acute Care hospital that was fairly close to Brenham. If I didn't have support and my advocate to fight for me it would have been awful. I knew the LORD was in my corner and HIS plan for me was to continue to be near family.

It was Michael's sister, Sandra, who actually found the Long Term Acute Care facility in New Braunfels. The facility was only 10 minutes from her house. Michael would be able to stay with her at night and spend the days with me. Insurance finally approved this location and transportation was finally arranged. I was to be discharged from the hospital on August 14 for the 2 ½ hour drive to New Braunfels. Abigail had come back for a visit on the 12th so she would be able to see the new facility.

I arrived at the new facility at 10 PM. This was a much later arrival than had been anticipated. I was supposed to have arrived by 7 but the transport ambulance was late picking me up. Michael had originally been told I would be in a private room, and that I would receive Physical and Occupational therapy a few times a week. Well, my first night there I was put in a room with another patient who had the TV blaring and streaming movies on her phone all night. I had never heard snoring like that either. The first nurse that came in to assess me said one of you is going to have to move. She immediately contacted the charge nurse to find another room for me. I was moved the next day to a room with another patient but she was quiet since she had a tracheotomy and was a quiet sleeper. I slept very well that next night. Of course, her alarms on her oxygen levels went off all night but it was much better than my first roommate.

It was probably my second or third day there when 2 physical therapists showed up to try and get me out of the bed and stand. Mind you this was mid-August and I had been confined in a hospital bed since July 10. Needless to say, my legs felt like limp spaghetti noodles with no strength at all. I could not stand. It was very disheartening to feel how weak I had become in such a short time. I did have to feed myself at this facility too. Aides would open containers and get things set up on the tray but I was expected to feed myself. It took forever at first but slowly I gained more confidence and strength to do it. I was on a soft chopped mechanical diet for the longest time. It wasn't until the last week I was there that I got a regular diet tray. What an improvement in the food at that point.

The case manager came in shortly after the physical therapists left that first time. She asked what my goals were. I told her the first one was to be able to stand and get to a bedside commode for my toileting. I did not have a catheter any longer and was using a pure wick device that soaked up the urine but I desperately needed some of my dignity back. She confirmed that it was a great goal and to work on baby steps. My second goal was to be able to get a shower and wash my hair. My first goal was met at the end of my first week. I worked hard with Physical Therapy (PT) whenever they came. My first accomplishment was to walk the length of the parallel bars which was about 6 steps. It was exhausting but it felt great! I gained strength in my legs and arms all week and by the end of the week I was able to sit on the edge of the bed and with assistance make it to the bedside commode. I was walking with a walker now during PT and also making progress on walking in the halls with my walker. My second goal came during my 2nd week there. The Occupational Therapist (OT) came in and worked with me on arm strength that first week usually right after PT. By the end of the second week, she said she was going to get me into the shower and wash my hair. Keep in mind that I had not had a shower or bed bath since entering the hospital on July 10. I was ready! When I arrived at the LTAC facility on August 14 I was using 10 liters of oxygen a minute to have saturation at 96-98%. The Respiratory Therapists here worked on tweaking my oxygen level down. Lowering the oxygen down is called titrating. This is done in small increments to see how the body will assimilate and tolerate the new level. In 3 weeks' time my oxygen needs were down to 3 ½ liters a minute in bed resting, but I still needed to crank up to 6 liters for PT or OT activities.

All of this was work. I was fighting to get back to the way I was before COVID-19. I had been totally independent of any oxygen or walking aides. I wanted to be able to go dancing again with Michael. I wanted to spend time with my kids and grandkids. All of them were my reason for fighting back. The LORD had spared me and I wanted to give back. The LTAC facility had a physical therapy side to it that they wanted to transfer me to. It would mean 5 days a week therapy for 3 hours a day. Typically, you need to be down to 2 liters of oxygen to go into the program, but they felt confident I would get there. They submitted paperwork, documentation of my progress from all therapies to my insurance company. Little did I know that our fight had only just begun.

Michael and I found out that my insurance company had outsourced the medical decisions to a third party company, Navicare. This company has a reputation for denying submissions/claims. Each time there is a submission there is up to a 72 hour waiting period. If there is a denial then you can appeal with a doctor to doctor appeal called a peer review which is another 72 hours for an answer. After that appeal there is a family appeal which again takes another 72 hours. Navicare just seemed to assume for some reason that I had been in poor health, used walking aids, and even oxygen use prior to COVID-19. I guess the assumption was my age; my salt and pepper hair I have no idea. The case worker at the LTAC had assumed the same thing prior to her assessment of me and getting my history.

I had been such a good fighter with the help of the LORD that I was denied on all levels of appeal because I was too healthy, I didn't need to see a doctor every day. I could go to a skilled nursing/nursing home to get the physical therapy I needed. Mind you those facilities only had high flow oxygen to 5 liters and I needed 6 liters for physical therapy. Also, in the fine print is they only approve for 20 days. I would need to reapply for more days and coverage would only be at 80%. I was now put in a position of not only fighting for my recovery but fighting with my insurance company. I knew from personal experience with parents on both sides of my family that a nursing home or skilled nursing facility was not for me. I would not have been able to get the necessary physical therapy to return to my prior level of function which was a totally independent woman.

I had to find the inner strength through my faith in GOD to stand up to the doctor over my care at the LTAC and tell him in no uncertain terms that I would not go to a skilled nursing/nursing home. I wanted to go home and have home health services. I needed a 10 liter oxygen concentrator and portable oxygen tanks. The case manager finally started working on that plan the Tuesday morning after Labor Day. She had waited till my insurance coverage was ending so these 72 hour appeals each time was being covered by insurance. They wanted me out.

The LORD and I certainly had our work cut out for us by Tuesday afternoon. Medicare portion of my insurance is the piece that will pay for equipment rental. They would only pay for a 5 liter oxygen concentrator and 4 portable tanks that only go to 5 liters as well. Even though all the documentation that they had received showed I needed 6 liters of oxygen for walking, physical therapy exercise, occupational therapy which included showering. The case manager knew what my needs were and I had to fight with the case manager to get a 10 liter concentrator.

Later that same afternoon the case manager came back with the Respiratory Therapist and a form from Medicare. The therapist explained to me that I would have to qualify for a 10 liter concentrator on a form from Medicare, that the documentation they had sent was not enough. She calmly explained what she and I would have to do in order to qualify. First, she would need to turn off my oxygen while I was lying in bed. She would have to time how long it took for my oxygen level to drop to a certain number (she didn't share what that number was). Second, she would turn my oxygen to 4 so I could recover, then I was to get up out of bed and use my walker to walk in the room back and forth for 6 minutes. As I was walking, she would again time how long it took for my oxygen to drop to a specific number then she would increase the oxygen a liter at a time for the duration of the 6 minutes.

It wasn't long before I heard her say I'm turning it to 5.... then 6.... then 7. As she said 7 it had only been 4 minutes and I told her I was getting light headed and dizzy. She instructed me to carefully come back to bed. The therapist actually had to turn my oxygen amount up to 10 liters for me to be able to recover to 90% and above. She wrote all over that Medicare form that I needed a 10 liter concentrator! The case manager took the form and went back to her office to contact Medicare. The entire time I was qualifying I felt the LORD's presence in the room, taking each step with me, taking each breath with me. My faith and trust in HIM brought me through again.

Michael had gone home Tuesday afternoon before I went through that whole qualifying process. The case manager had told him she wasn't sure she could get transportation for my trip home since it was 2 ½ hours away from New Braunfels. Michael saw our neighbor out in his yard who just happens to be the

Emergency Director for Washington County where we live. Michael asked him if he knew of a local transport company that could transport me back home from New Braunfels. He told Michael that because I am a resident of Washington County all EMS trips are free. Michael gave the case manager the contact information he received from our neighbor and she was able to get my transportation arranged for Wednesday afternoon at 4 PM on September 8, 2021.

I knew my fight to survive would continue after I went home and received home health services. This fight would not be over until I was free of any walking aid or oxygen. I wanted to be back to my prior level of function and just knew in my heart that I would get there with GOD's healing strength and power.

The LORD was with me through this fight. My faith in HIM gave me the strength to fight back health wise, to fight my insurance company, to fight for the ability to be here for my husband, children, step-children, grandchildren, and brothers. I give all the praise and glory to JESUS for this miracle and purpose for my life. My fighter hat has been on overload for myself and all members of my family.

I don't know how people can go through life without this faith, hope, and trust in the LORD. We are human with so many faults but with CHRIST all things are possible. HE loved us before we were even born and HE sent HIS only SON as our gift to eternal life. What better promise could there ever be than to believe and know that once you accept JESUS as LORD and SAVIOR of your life that you will live eternally and HE will be with you always with every step and breath that you take.

I AM: *A Survivor*

As I begin this final chapter there are 24 days till the end of 2021 and only 11 days till Christmas. My first night home to sleep in my own bed with my husband was September 8. Arrangements were made with my insurance for a 10 Liter oxygen concentrator and 1 portable oxygen tank with regulator and cart to come with me on the ambulance ride home. Michael named the big noisy concentrator R2D2. It was plugged in and ran 24/7 with it being moved to the front room at night so we could sleep and to the bedroom during the day so we could carry on conversations and hear the TV. We were both pretty nervous that first night using the 10 Liter oxygen concentrator by ourselves with no alarms if my level went to 88% or lower. When I first arrived home, I was on 3.5 Liters of oxygen a minute at rest and still needing 6 Liters for any activity like walking with my walker, Physical Therapy, Occupational Therapy, showering, dressing, etc.

It was nice not hearing alarms going off all night, but it was also nerve racking. At one point in the night, I woke up and thought it wasn't running correctly. I tapped Michael and he jumped out of bed and ran down the hall to check on it. Everything was perfectly fine. We both fell back asleep and woke up at our usual times. He got up around 7 and made coffee and I got up at 8. My tubing from R2D2 was 25 ft and my cannula tubing attached to it was 9 feet so I was able to get from the bedroom and bathroom to the living room easily. I went to the living room and sat in my usual spot on the couch. Michael had the news on and asked if I wanted a cup of coffee. I said yes and he brought me my mug that says "I couldn't have picked a better husband". He had his matching wife mug "I couldn't have picked a better wife". Michael sat down next to me on the couch and reached for my hand. He looked at me with tears in his eyes and said, "I really didn't think I would be able to do this again. Sit here with you in the morning, drink coffee, hold hands, and watch the news. It was our daily routine and I had missed it and you terribly while you were gone." I had never seen Michael tear up before. He had been such a rock for me this whole time. I squeezed his hand and kissed his cheek. I assured him I wasn't going anywhere and I was right where I wanted to be and was supposed to be. I told him I knew GOD had been healing me and restoring me to be here for him, for us, and that HE still had a purpose for me to fulfill. My survivor, wife, and faith hats were firmly in place.

When I first came home on September 8, I had mentally set a goal for myself; to be able to get around and do all activities on 4 Liters of oxygen. I had come home needing 3.5 Liters at rest and for walking with my walker or any kind of physical activity I needed to turn the level of oxygen to 6 Liters. I thought this was a pretty realistic goal and shared that goal with the RN (registered nurse) from the Home Health Company that came out to do my initial assessment on September 9, 2021. You will have to continue reading to see if I reach my goal.

The RN took my vitals, listened to my lungs as I breathed, got my list of medications, and took my pre-Covid history of being totally independent, no walking aids, no oxygen, drove my own car, went dancing with my husband, active with church and church activities, was in a book club that met monthly, etc. All of this pre- COVID independent history seemed to surprise her. She even questioned me again about not having any kind of walking aid or oxygen prior to COVID. She also took my COVID history including when I had tested positive and when I was admitted to the hospital. She wanted to know how long I had been on the ventilator and confined to bed. What my oxygen needs were at the beginning of COVID, as I left the hospital, and what oxygen needs I had while at the LTAC. The nurse was totally shocked at how well I was doing and how good I looked after hearing my story and being in a hospital setting from July 10-September 8. She has seen many post COVID patients and not one had been in as good a shape as I was. I gave GOD all the praise and glory and all the credit for my current condition. She documented my goal of being on a low enough level of oxygen at rest that I could do all activities and get the Christmas meal ready for my family only needing 4 Liters of oxygen. She thought that was a doable goal. She told me that a Physical Therapist would be coming the next day to do an assessment to set how many times a week I would see a physical therapist here in the home. I would also be assessed by an Occupational Therapist to determine those needs and how many times a week that would be necessary. A nurse would be coming by twice a week to check on me as well.

Ann, the assessment Physical Therapist came out the next morning. She was very pleasant and again mentioned how good I was looking. She assessed my leg strength, walking with my walker and my balance. We did some exercises lying in bed and sitting in a chair. She had me walk for 6 minutes on 6 liters of oxygen with my walker. I was only able to walk 75 feet in 6 minutes with resting that first time. My oxygen level had dropped to 80% and it took me 2 minutes to recover to mid-90's. She told me that I would be having PT twice a week with Angie. I would also have monthly re-evaluations by her to determine next steps and re-qualify for another month of insurance coverage for home health services. She had read the goal that I had given the nurse the day before. Ann concurred that it was a realistic and doable goal.

Sherita, the Occupational Therapist came the fol-lowing week and did her assessment. Her focus would be more of the daily care, hygiene, toileting, meal prep upper body strength work. It was not a good evaluation with her. I felt like I needed to perform for her for some reason. My normal routine for walking to the restroom would be to sit, recoup, then wash hands, recoup, and return to the living room. After she took my oxygen level and pulse rate, she told me to walk to the bathroom, sit on the toilet, get up and get into the shower and sit on the shower bench, then stand and walk to the sink, wash your hands, then after all of that walk back to the dining room to sit and retake the oxygen level and pulse rate. You should know I have a great poker face. She kept asking me if I was okay and I would smile and say yes. I had started this little journey at 95% oxygen pulse rate 115, when she took it again oxygen was 77% and pulse 140. All of her requirements were met on 6 liters of oxygen. Sherita was very upset and told me to never do that to her again. If I needed a break, I had to tell her. I told her I felt like I had to perform for her and she apologized if she had given me that impression. She said I had totally fooled her by my persona of not being in distress at all. I recovered and we set up a once a week schedule of when she would be coming back to the house.

On September 13 I began my PT with Angie. We set our schedule for Mondays and Fridays around 9 am. We began with a series of bed exercises with easy at first just pulling each leg to a bent position and down, then legs bent raising hips for those glute muscles, of laying on my side and doing leg lifts, sliding leg movements from a flat position (like the way you would make a snow angel with your legs); Angels, how appropriate! Using these muscles that had not been used for a few months now was painful and I needed all of my angels on board to get through these exercises. I also did my hip flexor muscle stretch on each side before getting up. Angie suggested I do these exercises on my own each day till she returned on Friday. I nodded okay. It was something constructive I could do to help in my recovery to get back to my prior level of function. My survivor hat was in place and working hard.

Thursday would be my OT day with Sherita. We started with some sitting arm exercises to increase my strength. These exercises consisted of bending arms from my lap to touch shoulders, from lap raising arms and tapping shoulders then raising hands, and stretching arms from chest to side. We also walked to the bathroom but only did one thing while there and walked back. I did much better with my oxygen numbers this time. She had me take my shoes and socks off and then put them back on. I had to sing while doing this so she could make sure I was breathing and not holding my breath. Zippidy Doodah Zippidy Day My Oh My What a Beautiful Day was the song I sang (whispered). I think my vocal cords may have been damaged by the ventilator tube. Seems like I have a laryngitis voice every day now.

I met my nurse this week as well for the first time her name is Melissa. She wanted to hear my COVID story as well. My vitals were good, lungs sounded good, and she was astonished at how good I looked and sounded. Both Michael and I asked for a tentative recovery time period to be back to prior level of function (pre-Covid life style). She could not give us a specific answer, everyone is different, still so many unanswered questions about COVID and its impact on the body. A general rule of thumb for people who have been hospitalized in general is for every day in the hospital a week for recovery. Oh my, I was in the hospital for 60 days which could mean 8 months for recovery or more. LORD, help me please!

September 20, I had a follow up appointment with my Primary Care Physician after my discharge from the LTAC. I was so nervous about going out on my portable oxygen tank and it lasting for the trip there, the appointment itself, and the trip home. Michael purchased a travel wheelchair and rigged up a backpack holder for the oxygen tank so I wouldn't have to walk using my walker and use up more oxygen doing it since I would need to crank it up to 5 liters. My PCP is in the same hospital system where I was cared for; so, she had access to all the tests, doctor notes, x-rays, etc. while I was here locally. I filled her in on the LTAC location; where it was, how long I was there, what my oxygen level was when I arrived and what it was when I left after 3 weeks. I told her what I had been able to accomplish in those 3 weeks during physical therapy and occupational therapy. I inquired if my husband and

I should get the vaccine now that both of us have had COVID. She shared that since I had such a bad case and my natural immune reaction to the treatments I had received; if she was in my shoes she didn't know if she would get it or not. If I chose to get the vaccine, she would recommend Moderna since there are fewer break through cases with that one. For her own notes she needed to turn off my portable oxygen tank and see how long it took me to get to 88%. It took less than 30 seconds so she knew I needed the oxygen and the rentals of the equipment monthly. I asked her to put in a referral for a Pulmonologist and set up my yearly labs and yearly checkup which she did.

Before I knew it a month had flown by and it was time for another PT evaluation from Ann. It was October 8 and we did the same things we had done for the initial assessment but this time I was only on 4 Liters for walking (without the use of my walker now) and OT activities and resting was now 3 Liters. Michael and I with the suggestions from Angie and PT successful days had been titrating my oxygen levels. This is lowering the Liters of oxygen in small increments and allowing the body to assimilate to the decrease. All of my leg strength exercises in the bed had improved as well as the sitting leg strengthening exercises. Now it was time for the 6 minute walk on 4 Liters of oxygen without my walker.

In just one month my 6 minute walk had improved from 75 ft to 550 ft. with a shorter rest break on just 4

Liters of oxygen without my walker. I dropped to 85% but climbed back to the mid 90's in 1 minute. Ann told me I had met my Christmas goal in just 1 month! Thank you, JESUS! Praise GOD. She was going to set a new goal for me; which was to be off all oxygen by the end of the year. Ann felt very strongly that I could do it. I had made huge gains in just one month and I had a Pulmonologist appointment scheduled for October and could ask him about this goal as well. My survivor hat was working!

My PT re-evaluation was on a Friday and I was still not getting out after a month of being home. I wasn't comfortable trying to go to church or life group or even the grocery store. I was still using 3 Liters of oxygen and the tanks would only last a total of 2-4 hours at that level of oxygen. Travel time and event time had to be calculated and it was still making me too nervous to venture out. That Sunday I started feeling sorry for myself. I was bored and feeling stuck inside the 4 walls of my house. I was sliding into a pity party depression. My faith hat had slipped a little.

That night as I laid in bed, I closed my eyes and said "Oh LORD I'm so sorry. YOU have done so much for me and I'm feeling sorry for myself. YOU breathed life into my lungs as I came off the ventilator." Silent hot tears slid from my eyes and poured down my cheeks. "When I needed strength to stand again, to walk again YOU were there. I am so sorry to have had this pity party for myself. LORD you have been healing me and are continuing to heal me daily. Thank you, JESUS, I give you all the praise and glory."

It was Monday morning again and Angie came for PT. We tried the stairs for the first time that day. We went half way up and back down. I used 3 Liters for climbing the stairs since it is more aerobic than the regular PT exercises that I was doing on only 2 Liters of oxygen. I only dropped to 88% and recovered to mid-90's in less than a minute. I walked back and forth from the dining room to the living room and the front door and oxygen didn't drop below 90%. I was only using 2 Liters to do this. I told Angie about my pity party the day before and my prayer to the LORD the night before. She said, "Well I would say this is an answer to your prayer. Go walk again." I did and oxygen stayed above 90%. My faith hat was back and securely in place again!

Sherita came for OT again and we did some exercises standing this time with the arm movements. She inquired about my dressing abilities, showering, toileting, and asked if I had any falls. It was at this visit that she learned I was able to dress myself without any assistance, I could sit on the shower seat and take my shower and Mike would wash my hair, getting to the bathroom and using the toilet was no problem and had not been since returning home. No falls to report and there never had been either pre or post COVID-19. Sherita felt strongly that she would be able to discharge me from OT services by the first of December. She would need to be here when I took a shower and did a meal prep, like make my salad for lunch since she came just before lunchtime each week. Mike and I decided that I could try and start washing my own hair to practice for the check off with Sherita. So, for the next full week until Sherita returned I was on my own in the shower.

The weeks continued to fly by and I kept getting stronger and stronger. Soon it was time for me to meet the Pulmonologist. My appointment was October 20. When he walked in, he shared with Michael and I that he had been the one to receive me the night in the ER when the helicopter life-flight brought me in. He commented on how well I looked and not nearly as sick as I had been when we first met. He took copious notes of my time at the LTAC, the starting oxygen levels, what I was on when I was sent home for home health to take over, and what was going on currently with my oxygen needs. I shared with him that I had met my first goal with home health in just one month. He also learned from me that they had set a new goal to be totally off oxygen by the end of the year and felt it was doable. He listened to me breathe several times but did not comment on the goal or the sound of my lungs. He did order a Pulmonary Function Test or PFT and a current chest x-ray for November 11. I would also have to take a COVID-19 test prior to the testing. I was hoping and praying it would not come back as a false positive since these tests were being done right at the 90 day mark post COVID.

I was feeling strong enough that I asked Mike if it would be okay to host our Life Group for dinner. I had not seen the whole group since going to the hospital back in July and it was now October 20,2021. These people had been praying for me, to breathe, to heal, and come back home. I just needed to be among my church family and thank them personally for their prayers and support. It was an awesome night of fellowship, sharing a meal, delving deeper into the message from the Sunday before, and giving a praise report on my progress. Mike and I were still not attending in person but we could listen to the sermon online.

My annual lab work and physical were way past due now so I scheduled my labs and follow up appointment with my Primary Care Physician for October 21 and November 4 respectfully. I continued with home health PT twice a week and OT once a week. The nurse visits went to 1 time a week. There was a big celebration on the horizon to be followed by 2 more huge family cele-brations and I wanted to know I was healthy and on track.

I had been in fight mode and survival mode for sev-eral months now and I wanted to share my successes with my family at my birthday celebration on Saturday October 30th. Mike was my chef for the day and he would prepare my favorite grilled chicken thighs, HEB potato salad, and make one of his scrumptious peach cobblers from scratch to be topped with Bluebell vanilla ice-cream. I shared with Angie and Sherita that week what my special plan was for the big day on Saturday.

Ben would be coming solo; Abby couldn't make it due to work and having traveled back so much over the summer and earlier in September. My brother Mark and his wife Kristin were tickled to come. Matt, Sarah, and Lucy would also be in attendance. Ally and Scarlett would have to come without Brandon since it was a Saturday and he had to work at the restaurant. My special plan was to greet all of my guests as they arrived without my cannula. I had been going without oxygen at rest for a few weeks by this point and felt I could do it. I told Angie and Sherita I would use my portable tank to get to the garage where the party would be held and check my oxygen level with my meter. If I needed a hit of oxygen, I would take one. I got a thumbs up from both of them! I could only be thinking about doing this because of my faith in the healing power of prayer and the LORD continuing to heal me and give me strength.

The Friday night before my birthday there was a little knock on our back door at 9pm. Michael answered it as I sat watching the TV. A tiny female voice said, "Hi" from behind me. I stood and turned to see my beautiful daughter Abigail beaming at me! She said, "Well look at you with no oxygen watching TV and standing to hug me!" I was totally in shock. Both Michael and Benjamin knew about this surprise visit for a month and had not mentioned a word about it. Abby just couldn't miss this special celebration of me, my life, my progress, and be given the opportunity to give all the praise and glory to HIM for the miracle that I was.

The birthday celebration was a huge success. Everyone was shocked and amazed to see me in the garage without being hooked up to my oxygen. Standing and hugging everyone as they arrived was the best feeling I had experienced in a long time. I did have to take 2 hits of oxygen that day but overall, from 11 in the morning till I went to bed at 10 that night I was without oxygen. Glory be to HIM for being with me every step and every breath that day. So many wonderful family memories were made that day. I am a survivor and wanted to share my life with my family. My family support and the relationships I have with each of them is what has kept me going. All of my hats were busy that day!

I truly believe I am a walking talking modern day miracle. GOD was not done with me here on earth and HIS purpose for me had not been fulfilled yet. My annual labs came back great. All my important numbers were good from A1C and thyroid to Cholesterol. The only number that was out of whack was my Vitamin D, it was way too high. Being too high can cause kidney stones and we for sure did not want that. My PCP asked me to stop taking the extra vitamin D that I had been taking and we would retest in January. The big question in the room was once again Immunity levels and COVID vaccines. When I asked her where I could get an antibody blood test she asked why? You had COVID you will have antibodies. At the same time, she said I should get the vaccine. Two months ago, she wasn't sure I should. What changed? I don't know. At this point it is still early November and my decision is still a no. I had too adverse a reaction to the treatments from my own natural immune system that I do not want to take a chance of that happening again to the vaccines and boosters.

At this appointment I shared with my PCP that my home health care team would like me to see a cardiologist since my pulse rate is still on the high end. She told me she would make a referral and their office would call me. She also ordered my mammogram and bone density test and a Cologuard kit. I also shared my wonderful oxygen free experience with my family for my birthday and in just two more weeks on November 14 we would be celebrating with 25 family members for an early Thanksgiving Thankfulness Celebration. She seemed genuinely happy for me. I felt so blessed with all of this positive news heading into my Pulmonary Function Test the following week.

Sunday November 7 was the first Sunday that Michael and I returned to church. It was also Communion Sunday which is an awesome way to celebrate my return and to celebrate the LORD for all HE has done for me and for Michael. Everyone was so glad to see me, hug on me, and tell me how much they love me. The music that Sunday during the Praise and Worship time was all about the healing power of JESUS. I remember during one of the songs two of my friends touched my back and held their hands on me for the duration of the song. After the service another friend came up and said she was so glad that they had done that. What she saw during that song was a light beaming down right over me whenever the words healing or healing power were sung. It just gave me goosebumps hearing that. I totally believe in the healing power of the LORD and the power of prayer where two or more are gathered. To me it was just another sign that GOD is in control.

I will be honest; I was a little nervous about this test for the Pulmonologist. I had looked it up on You tube and it didn't look pleasant. All 3 tests were to be done without oxygen while breathing through your mouth with your nose clipped shut. I am not a mouth breather and didn't know if I would be successful or not. I prayed to JESUS for strength and stamina the night before the test. I asked for good solid rest and sleep so I could be at my best the next day. The technician doing the test had me put my things and portable oxygen tank at a chair on the side of the room and walk to the testing booth. She explained each of the 3 tests before we started each one. She let me know that I would have to repeat each test until I had 2 tests with very similar numbers. Okay, well I had to do the first test like 6 times before she had her 2 similar test results. The next 2 tests I did a better job and only had to do them twice each. Thank you, LORD!! The final test would be a 6 minute walking test without oxygen. I chuckled to myself with that one. I remembered the qualifying test for the 10 liter concentrator and that had not been a huge success. She told me if my oxygen dropped to a certain level she would stop the test, put me on oxygen, and start the test over again. I asked her what the oxygen number had to drop to and she said 88%. I was very familiar with that number as my alarm was set to that at LTAC when I was on oxygen. The technician put my finger in the pulse-ox meter and it read out on a large screen I was to carry and show her upon my return from the end of the hall. One way down the hall was 25 feet. As I got to the end of the hall and turned to come back the screen read 88%. I called out the numbers as I walked toward her, 86% 84% 82% got to her and she read 80%. She told me sit down, she hooked me up to my portable oxygen tank and set it to 2 Liters which is what I was on when I came in. I was able to get my oxygen level up to 95% and we started again. I made 2 trips down and back before it dropped to 88%, she turned the oxygen to 3. I walked on 3 liters the rest of the time up till the last minute when it dropped to 88% again. She turned it to 4 liters for the last minute of the walk.

I sat down and she took my blood pressure 3 times till it was in better range, and the oxygen level was back up to 95%. The test results would be sent directly to the Pulmonologist and not put on the patient portal. The chest x-ray I had done before the PFT would be going on the portal and the Dr would write a summary of what he saw. The tests I had done with her would be gone over at our follow up appointment on January 12, 2022. She did tell me two very good things going in my favor. My required number of liters of oxygen is heading in the right direction which is down considerably from where I had started and I recover quickly when I dip to 88% oxygen. Both very good signs of recovery. The portal had a test result and the Pulmonologist had looked at the chest x-ray. He said it was much better and much improved from the last one he saw on July 30 while I was still in the hospital. Yes, another praise. Thank you, GOD!

It is just a few days from our Thankful Thanksgiving with family. Since we were celebrating on November 14 a Sunday, Brandon would be able to come with Allyson and Scarlett, Ben and his 5 boys came but Maria was sick. Both my brothers and their wives came. I had not seen Stephen since the day before the extubation. He also had not seen me without a cannula. What a look of pure joy on his face. My niece and her 3 girls and the oldest's boyfriend as well as Matt, Sarah, and Lucy were in attendance. Abigail let me purchase her a ticket to be here even though she had just been home for my birthday 3 weeks prior. Michael had helped me set up the garage with tables and chairs and decorations. I had prepped all the food items on Saturday for the girls to put in the oven Sunday since I cannot be by an operating gas stove or oven.

I said the prayer that day thanking them all for coming and sharing in this momentous day. I thanked them for loving me, supporting me, and praying for me in my fight to recover. I told them it was because of each one of them and the mighty power of GOD that I was here to celebrate this Thanksgiving with them this year.

It was a wonderful day of fellowship, eating, playing games, and making wonderful family memories. I wore all of my many hats that day and fell asleep that night with a smile on my face, having been oxygen free all day and never needing a hit like I had at my birthday celebration just 3 weeks before. The LORD was still healing me, thank you!

My PT and OT schedule continued throughout the month of November. Sherita said she would be graduating me and discharging me from home health services on December 2. I would do my meal prep and shower for final check off. Ann did her re assessment on November 29. I was working on 1.5 liters for walking and PT exercises as well as OT activities. When walking up the stairs I was still using 3 liters as it is more aerobic. Since the last week of October, I have been able to go all the way up the stairs and down without dropping below 88% oxygen. I could not believe my ears after the walking test. I did not take a rest break at all; I was on 1.5 Liters of oxygen and walked 875 ft. The oxygen level was cut in half from the month before and I walked an additional 25ft with no rest break!! All I could shout was thank you JESUS!! I am being healed in your name!

The Cardiologist appointment went very well. The doctor didn't see a reason for me to have come. He wasn't concerned about the pulse rate as I had a 90+ rate prior to COVID 19. The pulse number had been coming down steadily since being home. Walking and doing exercises would help reduce the pulse number. The EKG he did in the office was normal. He wanted to do an Echo-cardiogram to make sure there wasn't anything going on that he couldn't hear. I also have a follow up appointment in March of 2022 and he is hoping I will be off all oxygen by then so I can start walking and exercising.

The last month of the year has been a busy one. The Echo-cardiogram was normal no signs of damage of any kind. The valves are operating as they should and at a good function rate. December 2 Sherita did discharge me from OT services from the home health company and I had gone to seeing a nurse one time every other week. GOD has blessed me beyond measure these past 6 months.

On Monday December 6 I talked with Angie about getting an INOGEN G5 before I didn't qualify for home oxygen and insurance picking up the rental cost each month. Since I was only using 1 liter of oxygen for everything even walking up the stairs, I really didn't need to keep the 10 liter concentrator and all the portable tanks, regulator and cart. I wanted the 10 Liter concentrator to go to someone else who could really use it and needed it. The INOGEN would be much more portable and easier to get around with than the tanks and cart. She thought it would be a good idea since the goal was to be off oxygen by the end of the year anyway. I contacted my Pulmonologist office and explained the situation to ask if they would write a prescription for the INOGEN G5. Their response was a very positive yes ma'am! I called INOGEN and placed my order giving the doctor contact information for the prescription. INOGEN received the prescription from the Pulmonologist on December 7 and I had my INOGEN G5 on Saturday December 11. All the time GOD is good GOD is good all the time. This is an amazing piece of equipment. I am blessed financially to be able to afford to purchase it. Thank you, JESUS. I called the oxygen rental equipment company on Monday December 13 to make arrangements for them to come pick up all of their equipment. I had the Pulmonologist call and cancel the original order so I would not be AMA which means against medical advice.

Sunday December 12 would be our last family celebration of the year. All of the kids, in laws, and grandchildren would be coming for a meal and gift exchange. I made center pieces for the tables and bought red table cloths. Abigail and Adrian flew in Friday night December 10. Michael and I drove to Austin early and had dinner with Allyson and Scarlett before heading to the airport to pick them up. Mark and Kristin would be coming on Saturday December 11 to help with all the food prep for the kid and grandkid gathering on Sunday. I was able to have a one on one conversation with my brother Mark and give him his Christmas card with my special note that I had written to just him about our relationship and how important he is and was to my battle to be here. There was so much laughter and banter that day. We had a great meal mid-day and thoroughly enjoyed each other's company.

Allyson called Sunday morning at 7:30 to let us know she was sick, thought it was something she had eaten, but didn't want to take any chances around me. She is so thoughtful. People started arriving at 11 and continued to arrive until 2:00. It has been my tradition to get a card for each individual to open as part of their gift. This year I had written a personal note to each of them letting them know I love them, they are part of the reason I am here for them, and I wouldn't have missed this Christmas for anything. After everyone was seated, I passed out the cards and said they had to read their cards before any presents were passed out. Abigail asked if I was also going to pass out the Kleenex too. She knows me so well and how mushy I can get. I will admit there were a few teary eyes as I looked around. Several hugs came my way which was very appreciated. This is a very special day shared with very special people in my life. I thank you again JESUS for giving me this opportunity.

I love my family and my many hats that I wear around them. I would not have traded or given up celebrating with them this fall for my birthday, Thanksgiving, or Christmas. GOD has blessed me with healing and strength and increased my faith during this journey the last 6 months. I am a survivor and have never fallen into the victim mode in any of my life journey trials and tribulations. All of my hats are securely in place as I get closer to Christmas and the end of the year.

It is Christmas morning and I am experiencing my Christmas miracle! My life group had specifically prayed that I be off the oxygen by Christmas and the LORD heard that prayer. When I woke up Christmas morning, I felt strong, didn't feel a need for any oxygen as I turned off my INOGEN from my night time use of 1 Liter. I showered and got dressed, Michael and I exchanged our gifts and cards, I made breakfast of avocado toast and poached eggs. I had not been able to make Michael's favorite breakfast since before July 1. I walked around the house and felt for the first time like I was back! Michael and I had a very quiet day together and started a project of going through the 100's of CD's and discarding and organizing them for both the house and his music in the garage. This was Michael's way of starting with a clean slate, organizing our lives now that I was back. It was like the birthday puzzle I had put together. All of the pieces of our lives together had come together. Working on this project together was like the old days prior to COVID. We did everything together!

The day after Christmas again I woke up feeling strong and not needing oxygen. We got around and had our breakfast before heading out to church. I took my INOGEN with me but didn't feel a need for it to walk to the truck, or walk into the church, or at all during the service or walking out afterwards. The smiles and amens and hugs that I got that morning at church were numerous. All praise and glory go to my SAVIOR and LORD the ONE who healed me and has blessed me through this entire experience. The entire Christmas weekend I was off the oxygen except for sleeping at night and then only on 1 liter of oxygen.

Angie came to see me on Monday morning after Christmas. I told her about my Christmas miracle and her eyes twinkled behind her N95 mask. It was then that she told me that Ann who would be coming to do my re-evaluation on Wednesday December 29 had put in her notes for my team that she would be discharging me from PT services from the home health company. Angie said it was her last visit that day. We did the stairs without oxygen and all the standing exercises without oxygen. I only dropped to 88% and it jumped back to mid-90's in 30 seconds or less. She told me that Ann was going to recommend outpatient Pulmonary/ Respiratory workouts and would give me the name of the facility to give to my Pulmonologist on January 12, 2022. He should be able to write an order so insurance will pay for all or a portion of it. I have been so blessed in all areas of this experience and I continue to speak of HIS healing daily.

I will have one more PT re-evaluation this year on December 29. Ann will be here at 9:00 AM for her discharge of me from home health. I don't know if she will have me do a 6 minute walk or not but I am ready. I know the nurse is going to ask for a discharge from Home Health Services when she comes out the first week of January 2022. I also have my follow up Pulmonologist appointment on January 12,2022.

December 29 arrived and so did Ann. We did our normal leg strength tests and answered all the health questions. My blood pressure was a little elevated and my oxygen level was 91% on room oxygen. We began the 6 minute walk without oxygen. She told me to pace myself and take any breaks when I felt I needed one and she would check my oxygen level. I was able to do 5 laps or 250 ft in my hallway before I felt a need to take a standing break. My oxygen level had dropped to 84%. I stood and took several slow deep breaths before she checked again and I was good to go at 92% oxygen on room air. I had 2 more minutes to walk. I was able to complete it without any more breaks. My oxygen level only dropped to 88% in those 2 minutes and I had been able to walk a total of 650ft without oxygen!! We were both thrilled with this outcome. My blood pressure had also come down after my walk. Walking really does help your blood pressure and pulse rate! Ann shared with me the name of the facility that could provide cardio/pulmonary rehab in an outpatient setting which would also do monitoring of heart and oxygen as I worked through the exercises. There would be treadmills, bicycles, free weights, and more to strengthen and build my stamina. I shared with her that Michael and I are considering starting square dance lessons in mid-January as well. Ann thought that was an excellent idea! I will give all the information to my Pulmonologist on January 12 and hopefully get signed up for this outpatient rehab.

The day of my Pulmonologist appointment had finally arrived. It is the new year, January 12, 2022. Michael and I were very excited to go to this appointment and find out the results from the Pulmonary Function Test that I had taken back in November. So many things had changed since then with my oxygen needs; to being discharged from home health services. Since I still need to wear a mask to doctor appointments, I decided to use my INOGEN on 1 Liter to help with breathing since I didn't know how long the wait or the appointment would be. I can breathe unaided and unmasked at a normal 95-96% oxygen levels. My INOGEN would just give me a little boost to be able to breathe easier and not inhale the carbon dioxide put out into my mask with every exhale of my breath.

The doctor came in and commented how well I was looking. He pulled up a side by side view of the chest x-ray from July 30 and the one done on November 11. He explained the significant changes and improvements from one over the other. He then started going over the 3 PFT test results. The first test measured how long I could exhale my breath. It was just over 6 seconds and the scale went to 8 so his comment was that was pretty good and compared to women my age without any lung issues. It could improve over time and with exercise and stamina increasing for deeper breaths and exhales.

The other two tests measured how much I was able to exhale from my inhale breaths. Both of these were only showing at 49-50%, these were not as good. It was at this point that he told me he wanted a CT scan to see if I had scaring in my bronchial tubes or any of the air sacs in the lungs had just collapsed on themselves. Many people do fine with the numbers that I showed back in November. I then shared with him the discharge from home health and their recommendation of outpatient cardio/pulmonary rehab. He thought this was an excellent idea and would definitely show up in a positive way with a follow up PFT test. He would put the orders in immediately for the outpatient rehab workouts to begin.

After this part of the appointment, I shared the reason I was using oxygen that day in the office. I told him I don't use oxygen during the day and average between 93%-96% oxygen throughout the day at room oxygen levels. I also made him aware that I use the INOGEN set at 1 liter for night time sleeping. I compared for him my 6 minute walking test without oxygen on November 11 during part of my PFT and only being able to walk 25 ft before dropping to 88% and then my discharge from home health 6 minute walking test without oxygen on December 29 and being able to walk 650 ft. His "Wow, that is a huge improvement in a month" warmed my heart. My survivor hat was working as well as my fighter and faith hats.

The last question I had for the Pulmonologist was a sleep study question to determine if I needed to sleep with oxygen at night. He agreed that it would be a good idea. He explained the entire procedure for that and it would be done right there in their clinic. He then listened to my lungs as I took deep breaths and normal breaths and he used the word excellent after listening. I was so excited. I looked at Michael and his eyes were twinkling above his mask.

The doctor wrote orders for the outpatient rehab, the CT scan, a PFT, and sleep study to be followed up with an office visit with him May 16, 2022. The orders are good till mid-April. I told the checkout gal I wanted to wait and schedule my tests after I had been to rehab and working out for a few months. That was no problem and she totally understood that and thought it was a great idea. Michael and I left with our summary of the visit with the tests listed and when they needed to be scheduled by. I felt relieved, happy, full of joy and thankfulness to my LORD for this good report.

We are looking forward to weekend getaways with friends and family, more grandchildren, and more family gatherings to stay blended as we have become. Michael and I are planning projects together for our home and our lives together. Our future is bright now and no limits to what we can experience together. We enjoy the simply things like holding hands, drinking coffee, or taking a golf cart ride together. Just to be able to look at each other and say I love you is a blessing from GOD.

I have now come to the end of my book but never the end of my faith journey. I wear my hats proudly. My hats of a woman of faith, being a wife, a mother, a step-mother and mother-in-law, a sister, a grandmother, a warrior, a fighter, and a survivor are still firmly in place never to be removed. As I said at the start, we wear our hats multiple times a day and change from one to the other without blinking an eye. I will not grow weary I will continue to pray, to fight for my family, to fight for my health, and never become a victim of anything that life may throw me. I will always overcome with the help of JESUS and be a survivor for life.

My prayer before writing this book and having it published was to be an encouragement of hope for others going through struggles in their lives. Have you identified the hats you wear? How do these hats give you strength? May your faith hat be the largest and most beautiful hat with all the answered prayers displayed as beautiful flowers with petals of words that have encouraged you, honored you, and blessed you beyond measure. Above all be a survivor in life by leaning on HIM.

About the Author

I am a mature Christian woman who has relied on my many hats and faith throughout my life. I was an elementary school teacher for 40 years in the public school systems of Indiana, Nebraska, and Texas. I am married to Michael, the most amazing husband in the world. We are living our retired years in the small community of Brenham, Texas in the home we built together. I am enjoying being able to participate in Church activities, Life Group, helping with Grandchildren, and maybe even learn how to square dance. I enjoy hosting game nights and having good fellowship over a meal with the many friends we have made here in Brenham. All of my grown kids will now be together in one state, the great state of Texas when Abigail and her boyfriend move back home in February of 2022.

CPSIA information can be obtained
at www.ICGtesting.com
Printed in the USA
LVHW081659180422
716540LV00014B/397